Managing Anxiety Workbook for Teens

A TOOLBOX of REPRODUCIBLE ASSESSMENTS and ACTIVITIES for FACILITATORS

Ester R.A. Leutenberg
and John J. Liptak, EdD

publisher of therapy, counseling, and self-help resources

Duluth, Minnesota

Managing Anxiety Workbook for Teens

publisher of therapy, counseling, and self-help resources

101 West 2nd Street, Suite 203
Duluth, MN 55802

800-247-6789

books@WholePerson.com
WholePerson.com

Managing Anxiety Workbook for Teens
A Toolbox of Reproducible Assessments and Activities
for Facilitators.

Copyright ©2016 by Ester R.A. Leutenberg and John J. Liptak.
All rights reserved. The activities, assessment tools, and handouts in this book are reproducible by the purchaser for educational or therapeutic purposes. No other part of this book may be reproduced or transmitted in any form by any means, electronic or mechanical without permission in writing from the publisher.

All efforts have been made to ensure accuracy of the information contained in this book as of the date published.

The author(s) and the publisher expressly disclaim responsibility for any adverse effects arising from the use or application of the information contained herein.

Printed in the United States of America

10 9 8 7 6 5 4 3 2 1

Editorial Director: Carlene Sippola
Art Director: Mathew Pawlak

Library of Congress Control Number: 2016937567
ISBN: 978-157025-346-1

Introduction

Using the *Managing Anxiety Workbook for Teens*

Teens experience stress about a great number of situations and circumstances, and anxiety is a normal reaction to stress. For teens, such circumstances as speaking in public, moving to a new neighborhood, dating issues, taking tests, making good grades, and competing in athletic events may all cause stress. For some teens various circumstances or events can cause more than the usual amount of stress. This leads to anxiety.

Anxiety has been defined as a state of intense apprehension, uncertainty, and fear resulting mainly from the anticipation of a threatening event or situation, often to a degree that disrupts normal, everyday physical and psychological functioning. Fear is an emotional response to a <u>real or perceived threat</u>. Anxiety is anticipation of a future threat.

Anxiety is normal in the everyday life of all people and can actually be a good thing. Anxiety motivates one to accomplish goals and warns a person of a dangerous situation. However, intense anxiety can involve debilitating symptoms and affect performance in school, athletics, and interpersonal interactions. Some teens persistently experience excessive amounts of worry and fear about everyday situations and this may lead to depression. Persistent anxiety and fear can interfere with daily activities. Often, these symptoms are difficult to control.

How Does Anxiety Manifest Itself?

Anxiety affects one's general well-being and manifests itself physiologically, behaviorally, and psychologically. Following are some of the ways that anxiety can affect teens:

- Apprehension
- Chills
- Cold or sweaty hands and/or feet
- Difficulty concentrating
- Dizziness
- Dry mouth
- Emotional tension
- Fear of anticipation of the worst outcome
- Feeling as if one's mind has gone blank
- Feelings of powerlessness
- Feelings of extreme fear
- Heart palpitations
- Inability to act
- Inability to express oneself
- Inability to sit or stand still
- Inability to sleep and/or remain asleep
- Inexplicable feelings of dread
- Irritability
- Jittery feelings
- Muscle tension
- Nausea
- Over-alertness for signs of danger
- Panic attacks
- Mind racing
- Shortness of breath
- Tingling of hands and/or feet

This Workbook has Two Goals

1. Our goal is NOT to diagnose a mental illness, or even for the facilitator to make that diagnosis from this workbook's content. Our goal is to touch on some of the symptoms and possibilities, create realizations, and provide coping methods which will help teens to go forward and perhaps consider the possibility of the need for medications and therapy.
2. Our other goal is to help participants recognize that other people have the same issues. No shame should be connected to them, nor should mental health issues of any kind be stigmatized

> In this workbook, we are using the phrase MENTAL HEALTH ISSUES to include all types of anxiety issues, from experiencing a few anxiety problems to serious, extremely intense anxiety issues.

"Normal" Anxiety vs. Intense Anxiety Disturbances

Anxiety is an inevitable part of everyday life for most teens. Some anxiety is actually an appropriate emotional response to a variety of situations that people encounter. The assessments and activities in this workbook can be valuable tools for helping teens deal effectively with "normal" everyday anxiety that they experience, as well as more intense anxiety disturbances.

Anxiety manifests itself in the everyday life of most teens in many different ways.

Some of the most common types of everyday, "normal" anxiety:
- **Situational Anxiety** – Feelings of apprehension and dread related to a specific situation such as taking a class in physics, moving to a new community, or trying out for the soccer team at school.
- **Anticipatory Anxiety** – Feelings of apprehension and dread when one confronts something that has been frightening in the past, or that has resulted in a negative experience such as speaking in front of classmates.

Anxiety Disturbances – These can be distinguished from the everyday, "normal" anxiety because they are more intense (panic attacks), last longer (often months or years instead of going away after an anxiety-producing situation), and interfere with a person's ability to function effectively in daily life (i.e., afraid to go to school, fear of getting bullied, etc.).

Different types of disturbances related to thinking and behavior are conveyed and expressed in different forms:
- **Panic Disorder:** Teens have feelings of extreme terror that strike suddenly and often without any warning. Teens with a panic disorder often experience sweating, chest pain, and/or heart palpitations. They feel as if they are out of control during one of their attacks of fear, and they attempt to avoid places where panic attacks have occurred in the past.
- **Social Anxiety Disorder:** Teens have feelings of overwhelming worry and experience extreme self-consciousness in everyday social situations. These worries include fear that others will judge them harshly, they will do something that may be embarrassing, and they fear being ridiculed by other teens. Teens with this disorder often are very anxious around other people and have a difficult time talking to others. They will stay away from places where there are other people and have a hard time making and keeping friends. This can lead to avoidance and selective mutism.
- **Generalized Anxiety Disorder:** Teens exhibit excessive, extreme, and/or unrealistic worry and tension, even if there is nothing (or very little) to be worried and/or tense about. Teens with this disorder may be worried about just getting through the day and doing everyday tasks. They often have trouble falling and staying asleep, relaxing, and concentrating in school.
- **Specific Phobias:** Teens experience intense, unwarranted fears about an object or a situation. The fear involved in a phobia is usually inappropriate for the phobia-producing object or situation and may cause people to avoid specific everyday activities in order to avoid the object or the situation. Some common phobias include snakes, speaking in public, clowns, fear of situations where escape from bad things is perceived as difficult. Phobias are intense fears resulting from real or imagined exposure to a wide range of situations.
- **Post-Traumatic Stress Disorder (PTSD):** Teens experience anxiety caused by exposure to traumatic events (i.e., child abuse, abandonment, accident, house fire, loss, victim of crime).
- **Anxiety Disorder Due to Another Medical Condition:** Teens experience anxiety attacks directly attributed to an existing medical condition (i.e., cancer diagnosis), and it often parallels the course of the illness.
- **Obsessive-Compulsive Disorder:** Teens have repetitive thoughts that will not dissipate (obsessions) and/or engage in ritual behaviors to dispel anxiety (compulsions).

Introduction

Which Teens are at Risk?

Many risk factors or things that might make teens more vulnerable or sensitive to experiencing anxiety have been identified. Some of these risk factors include genetic factors such as living in a family with a history of mental health issues; personality factors such as high sensitivity or extreme introversion; environmental factors, such as experiencing ongoing stress or a single stressful event that occurs in the teen's life; and medical factors such as ongoing physical illness.

When to Worry?

Symptoms related to intense anxiety can be very complex and difficult to cope with. The good news is that teens can develop the skills needed to manage the symptoms and progress forward to begin enjoying life more. Undergoing the stress that accompanies many of the mental health issues can be a very frightening way to live. **A teen who experiences anxiety and stress over time is at risk of developing a serious mental or physical illness and needs to seek a medical professional.**

Suicide Warning!

People who experience intense anxiety may feel suicidal, harbor suicidal thoughts, and plan to die by suicide. Sometimes they think that the only way to escape the physical, psychological, and emotional pain is suicide. Remember to take any talk about suicide or suicidal acts very seriously.

Signs of Suicidal Thoughts

- Calling or visiting people to say goodbye
- Drastic changes: angry person becoming super happy, style of clothes, shaving head
- Dropping out of school
- Engaging in reckless actions
- Expressing feeling of being trapped with no way out
- Expressing severe hopelessness about the future
- Giving away possessions
- Increasing use of harmful substances
- Making a plan for dying by suicide
- Purchasing a weapon
- Talking about harming oneself or another person
- Withdrawing from family, friends, and activities of interest in the past

Serious Mental Illness

If participants have a serious mental illness, they need to do much more than complete the assessments, activities and exercises contained in this workbook. They need to be taken seriously and facilitators can take an active role in their finding help immediately. All disturbances related to intense anxiety need to be thoroughly evaluated by a medical professional and then treated with an appropriate combination of medication and group and/or individual therapy.

Format of the *Managing Anxiety Workbook for Teens*

The *Managing Anxiety Workbook for Teens* is designed to be used either independently or as part of an established mental health issue program. You may administer any of the assessments and the guided self-exploration activities to an individual or a group with whom you are working, and you may administer any of the assessments and activities over one or more days. Feel free to pick and choose those that best fit the outcomes you desire. The purpose of this workbook is to provide facilitators who work with individuals and groups who may be experiencing anxiety issues with a series of reproducible activities that can be used to supplement their work with participants. Because these activity pages are reproducible, they can be photocopied as is, or you may adapt them by whiting out and writing in your own changes to suit the needs of each group, using that page as your master copy to be photocopied for each participant.

Assessments

Assessments establish a behavioral baseline from which facilitators and participants can gauge progress toward identified goals. This workbook will supplement the facilitator's work by providing assessments designed to measure client change in those behavioral baselines. In order to do so, assessments with scoring directions and interpretative materials begin each module. The authors recommend that you begin presenting each topic by asking participants to complete the assessment. Facilitators can choose one or more or all of the activities relevant to their participants' specific needs and concerns.

Each of the awareness modules contained in this workbook begin with an assessment for these purposes:
- To assist participants to feel a part of the treatment planning process.
- To help facilitators gather valuable information about their participants.
- To help facilitators identify patterns that are negatively affecting participants.
- To help facilitators in the measurement of change over time.
- To help facilitators to develop a numerical baseline of behavior, attitude, and personality characteristics of participants before they begin their individual treatment plans.
- To prompt insight and behavioral changes in participants' lives.
- To provide participants with a starting point to begin to learn more about themselves and their strengths and limitations.
- To use as pre-tests and post-tests to measure changes in behavior, attitude, and personality.

Assessments are a great aid in developing plans for effective change. Be aware of the following when administering, scoring, and interpreting the assessments in this workbook:
- The purpose of these assessments is not to pigeonhole people, but to allow them to explore various elements of themselves and their own situations.
- This workbook contains self-assessments and not tests. Traditional tests measure knowledge or right or wrong responses. For the assessments provided in this workbook, remind participants that there are no right or wrong answers. These assessments only ask for opinions or attitudes.
- The assessments in this workbook have face value, but have not been formally normed for validity and reliability.
- The assessments in this workbook are based on self-reported data. In other words, the accuracy and usefulness of the information is dependent on the information that participants honestly provide about themselves. Assure them that they do not need to share their information with anyone. They can be honest!
- Remind participants that the assessments are exploratory exercises and not a judgment of who they are as human beings.
- The assessments are not a substitute for professional assistance. If you feel any of your participants need more assistance than you can provide, refer them to an appropriate medical professional.

(Continued on the next page)

Introduction

Format of the *Managing Anxiety Workbook for Teens* (Continued)

Assessment Script

When administering the assessments contained in this workbook, please remember that the assessments can be administered, scored, and interpreted by the client. If working in a group, facilitators should circulate among participants as they complete assessments to ensure that there are no questions. If working with an individual client, facilitators can use the instruction collaboratively.

Please note that as your participants begin the assessments in this workbook, the participants' instructions italicized below are meant to be a guide, so please do not feel you must say them word for word.

Tell your participants: *You will be completing a quick assessment related to the topics we are discussing. Please remember that assessments are powerful tools if you are honest with yourself. Be truthful in your responses so that your results are an honest reflection of you. Your level of commitment in completing the assessments honestly will determine how much you learn about yourself.*

Allow participants to turn to the first page of their assessment and read the instructions silently to themselves. Then tell them: *All of the assessments have similar formats, but they have different scales, responses, scoring instructions, and methods for interpretation. If you do not understand how to complete the assessment, ask me before you turn the page to begin.*

Then tell them: *Before completing each assessment, be sure to read the instructions. Because there is no time limit for completing the assessments, take your time and work at your own pace. Do not answer the assessments as you think others would like you to answer them or how you think others see you. These assessments are for you to reflect on your life and explore some of the barriers that are keeping you from living a more satisfying life.*

Make sure that nobody has a question, then tell them: *Learning about yourself can be a positive and motivating experience. Don't stress about taking the assessments or discovering your results. Just respond honestly and learn as much about yourself as you can.*

Tell participants to turn the page and begin answering with Question 1. Allow sufficient time for all participants to complete the assessment. Answer any questions. As people begin to finish, read through the instructions for scoring the assessment. Have participants begin to score their assessment and transfer their scores for interpretation. Ask if anyone has questions about how to do the scoring.

Review the purpose of the interpretation table included after each assessment. Tell the participants: *Remember, this assessment was not designed to label you. Rather, it was designed to develop a baseline of your behaviors. Regardless of how you score on an assessment, consider it a starting point upon which you can develop healthier habits. Take your time, reflect on your results, and note how they compare to what you already know about yourself.*

After participants have completed, scored, and interpreted their assessment, facilitators can use the self-exploration activities included in each module to supplement their traditional tools and techniques to help participants function more effectively.

(Continued on the next page)

Format of the *Managing Anxiety Workbook for Teens* (Continued)

Self-Exploration Activities

This workbook will provide self-exploration activities that can be used to reduce stress and decrease anxiety. These activities, included after each of the modules, will prompt self-reflection and promote self-understanding. They use a variety of formats to accommodate all learning styles, foster introspection, and promote pro-social behaviors, life skills, and coping skills. The activities in each module correlate to the assessments to enable you to identify and select activities quickly and easily.

Self-exploration activities assist participants in self-reflecting, enhancing self-knowledge, identifying potential ineffective behaviors, and teaching more effective ways of coping with anxiety. They are designed to help participants make a series of discoveries that lead to increased social and emotional competencies, as well as to serve as an energizing way to help participants grow personally and professionally. These brief, easy-to-use self-reflection tools are designed to promote insight and self-growth.

Many different types of guided self-exploration activities are provided for you to pick and choose the activities that are most needed by your participants and the ones that will be most appealing to them. The unique features of the exploration activities make them user-friendly and appropriate for a variety of individual sessions and group sessions.

In some activities, participants will have the opportunity to engage in these ways:
- Explore how they could make changes in their lives to feel better. These activities are designed to help participants reflect on their current life situations, discover new ways of living more effectively, and implement changes in their lives to accommodate these changes.
- Journal as a way of enhancing their self-awareness. Through journaling prompts, participants will be able to write about the thoughts, attitudes, feelings, and behaviors that have contributed to, or are currently contributing to, their current life situation. Through journaling, participants are able to safely address their concerns, hopes, and dreams for the future.
- Explore their intense anxiety issues by examining their past for negative patterns and learning new ways of dealing with them more effectively in the future. These activities are designed to help participants reflect on their lives in ways that will allow them to develop healthier lifestyles.

Take-Away Skills

Take-Away Skills for each Module Following each Cover Page
Conditions and Behavior, Frequency and Duration, and/or Accomplishment statements for each activity may be used in educational and/or treatment planning. They may also be used to measure progress toward goals. These skills promote real life outcomes and behavioral changes.

Introduction

The Stigma Awareness Approach

It is important that facilitators keep an open mind about mental health issues and the stigma attached to people experiencing these issues. Rather than thinking of people as having a mental disorder, or being mentally ill, the *Erasing the Stigma of Mental Health Issues through Awareness* series is designed to help facilitators diminish the stigma that surrounds people suffering from intense anxiety issues. Stigmas occur when people are unjustly labeled, thus setting the stage for discrimination and humiliation. Facilitators are able to help to erase the stigma of mental illness through enhancing awareness of the factors that activate and accentuate the depth of the issues, and thereby accelerate awareness and understanding.

To assist you, a module titled *Erasing the Stigma of Mental Health Issues* is included to provide activities to help erase the stigma associated with intense anxiety issues.

The Awareness Modules

The reproducible awareness modules contained in this workbook will help you identify and select assessments and activities easily and quickly:

Module I: Signs of Stress Symptoms
   This module will help participants explore the signs of stress in their lives, recognize the symptoms of anxiety, and learn tools to begin to help decrease the anxiety.

Module II: Need for Control
   This module will help participants explore the various ways they need to be in control of their lives.

Module III: Social Approval
   This module will help participants explore the various ways that their need for the approval of others affects their functioning in social situations.

Module IV: Perfectionism
   This module will help participants explore ways that their need to be perfect and mistake-free, and their determination to achieve unrealistic standards can cause anxiety.

Module V: Erasing the Stigma of Mental Health Issues
   This module will help participants explore the stigma of having intense anxiety and the impact that the stigma has on them.

How the *Managing Anxiety Workbook for Teens* Can Help

Teens who experience intense anxiety are likely to find it difficult to function in everyday life due to the symptoms associated with anxiety. The assessments and activities in this workbook are designed to provide facilitators with a wide variety of tools to use in helping people manage the intense anxiety in their lives more effectively. Many choices for self-exploration are provided for facilitators to determine which tools best suit the unique needs of their clients.

The purpose of this workbook is to provide a user-friendly guide to short-term assessments and activities to help teens manage their anxiety and the stress that often triggers it, and to give them a greater sense of well-being. In addition, this workbook is designed to help provide facilitators and participants with tools and information needed to overcome the stigma attached to intense anxiety issues.

In order to help participants cope successfully with stress and the subsequent anxiety, facilitators need to have a variety of assessments and activities to help their participants open-up and begin to feel as if they can manage their anxiety to begin living a more calm and peaceful life. The Managing Anxiety Workbook for Teens provides assessments and self-guided activities to help participants understand the intensity of their issues and how they can lead more effective lives.

Confidentiality

Instruct teens to use NAME CODES when writing or speaking about anyone.
Teens completing the activities in this workbook might be asked to respond to assessment items and journal about their anxiety. Before you begin using the materials in this workbook explain to teens that confidentiality is a term for any action that preserves the privacy of other people. Maintaining confidentiality is extremely important as it shows respect for others and allows – even encourages – teens to explore their feelings without hurting anyone's feelings or fearing gossip, harm or retribution.

In order to maintain this confidentiality, ask teens to assign a NAME CODE for each person they write about as they complete the various activities in the workbook. For example, a friend named **Joey** who **enjoys going to hockey games** might be titled **JLHG** (Joey Loves Hockey Games) for a particular exercise. In order to protect their friends' identities, they will not use people's actual names or initials, just NAME CODES.

Our thanks to these professionals who make us look good!

Art Director	—	Mathew Pawlak
Editorial Director	—	Carlene Sippola
Editor and Lifelong Teacher	—	Eileen Regen, M.ED., CJE
Reviewer	—	Jay Leutenberg, CASA
Reviewer	—	Carol Butler, MS Ed, RN, C
Reviewer	—	Niki Tilicki, MA Ed

Table of Contents

Module I – Signs of Stress Symptoms 17
Take-Away Skills Emphasized in Each Activity Handout 18-20
Signs of Stress Symptoms Introduction and Directions 21
Signs of Stress Symptoms Scale P 22
Signs of Stress Symptoms Scale E 23
Scoring Directions 24
Profile Interpretation 24
Scale Descriptions 24
Stress in My School Life 25
Stress Associated With My Relationships 26
My Stress Triggers 27
A Past Stressful Situation 28-30
Picturing My Stress – NOW and THEN 31
Worry Work 32
Worry Self-Talk 33
Recognizing High Anxiety Situations 34
My Anxiety Situations 35
Anxiety Tension 36
Effects of Anxiety 37
You Have Been Asked … 38
Basic Anger Management Tools 39
My Coping Strategies 40
Quick Meditation 41
My Kryptonite 42

Table of Contents

Module II – Need for Control 43
    Take-Away Skills Emphasized in Each Activity Handout 44-45
    Need for Control Scale Introduction and Directions.....................47
    Need for Control Scale 48
    Scoring Directions 49
    Profile Interpretation 49
    Scale Descriptions..49
    Control or Not? 50
    Changes in My Life 51
    My IF Fears...52
    Go to Your Fears..53
    Doodling 54
    Taking Action to Reduce Anxiety 55
    Over and Over and Over Again!..56
    Hocus-Focus 57
    What's the Worst Thing? 58
    From a Self-Fulfilling Prophecy to Imagining the Best.................59
    Staying in the Present 60
    Deep Breathing 61
    Relaxing Your Body..62
    Mindfulness 63
    Mindfulness Journaling 64

Table of Contents

Module III – Social Approval 65
    Take-Away Skills Emphasized in Each Activity Handout 66-67
    Social Situation and Social Perception Scales
        Introduction and Directions 69
    Social Situation Scale 70
    Social Perception Scale 71
    Scoring Directions 72
    Profile Interpretation 72
    Scales' Descriptions 72
    Events Where I Feel Anxious 73
    People with Whom I Feel Anxious 74
    Situations in Which I Feel Anxious 75
    Ways I Avoid Social Situations 76
    Social Situations Realities 77
    Need for Approval 78
    Validation 79
    I'm Good Enough! 80
    Rejection, Abandonment, and Disapproval 81
    Challenge Negative Thinking 82
    Ways Thinking Can Be Debilitating 83
    Positive Self-Talk Scripts 84
    Meet New People 85
    Self-Appreciation 86
    Accepting ME 87

Table of Contents

Module IV – Perfectionism 89
Take-Away Skills Emphasized in Each Activity Handout............... 90-91
Perfectionism Scale Introduction and Directions 93
Perfectionism Scale 94
Scoring Directions 95
Profile Interpretation 95
Scale Descriptions.. 95
Criticizing Myself.. 96
Criticizing Others 97
Handling Criticism from Others.. 98
Perfectionistic Thinking 99
How I Feel When I am Being a Perfectionist........................... 100
Perfectionistic Thoughts... 101
I Must be Perfect 102
Perfectionism Affirmations 103
A Perfectionistic Contract 104
The Good and the Bad 105
Underlying Perfectionistic Reasons 106
Small Steps in Setting Realistic Goals............................... 107
My Perfectionistic Moments 108
Respecting and Loving Myself 109
The Positive Me 110

Introduction

Table of Contents

Module V – Erasing the Stigma of Mental Health Issues 111
- Erasing the Stigma of Mental Health Issues Introduction...............112
- Two Types of Mental Health Stigma.....................................113
- The Stigma of Intense Anxiety – THE PAST............................114
- The Stigma of Intense Anxiety – THE PRESENT........................115
- Speak Your Mind 116
- If We Stamp Out the Stigma … 117
- Glenn Close said … 118
- Effects of Anxiety Issues 119
- The Stigma of Going to a Mental Health Therapist 120
- Will You Speak Out? 121
- My Negative Thoughts 122
- Focus on Your Strengths...123
- Ways I Try to Minimize My Anxiety Issues............................124
- Ways I am Treated 125
- Self-Doubt..126
- A Poster about the STIGMA of People Who Experience Anxiety 127
- A Poster about ACCEPTANCE of People Who Experience Anxiety.......128
- DE-STIGMA-TIZE with the Facts about Mental Health Issues............129
- Coping with the Stigma of an Intense Anxiety Issue 130
- A Letter to the Editor 131

MODULE I

Signs of Stress Symtoms

Anxiety's like a rocking chair. It gives you something to do, but it doesn't get you very far.

~ Jodi Picoult

Name _____

Date _____

Managing Anxiety Workbook for Teens

Module I – Take-Away Skills

We have included skills for most of the handouts in each Module, *Conditions and Behavior* (1), *Frequency and Duration* (2), and/or *Accomplishment* (3) statements for each activity may be used in educational and/or treatment planning, and also used to measure progress toward goals. These Take-Away skills promote real life outcomes and behavioral changes. Feel free to add additional skills for each activity.

Examples

1. **Conditions and Behavior** – a skill or healthy habit to replace a previous less effective behavior/habit.
   - Now, I … *(less effective or undesired behavior)*
     when I … *(when do I do this?)*.
     Instead I will … *(more effective or desired new behavior)* in ___ out of ___ opportunities.
2. **Frequency and Duration** – a skill or healthy habit not necessarily tied to a condition or previous behavior.
   - I will *(describe the behavior)* _____ times per _____.
3. **Accomplishment** – an outcome that is a one-time accomplishment.
   - I will *(describe the accomplishment)* by _____ *(date)*.

Take-Away Skills Examples

Stress in My School Life 25
Conditions and Behavior
- Now, I … *become short-tempered*
  when … *I don't feel my opinion is valued during group work.*
  Instead I will … *share my feelings using an I-statement in 4 out of 4 opportunities.*
- Now, I … *avoid going to the after-school program*
  when … *I know someone who bullies me will be there.*
  Instead I will … *talk to a teacher about my concerns and attend in 4 out of 4 opportunities.*
- Now, I … *feel tense in my shoulders*
  when … *I have to take a test.*
  Instead I will … *take some deep breaths and repeat "I can do this" to myself in 4 out of 4 opportunities.*

Stress Associated with Relationships 26
Conditions and Behavior
- Now, I … *say "yes"*
  when I … *am asked to do something I don't really want to do.*
  Instead I will … *definitively say no 4 out of 4 opportunities.*
- Now, I … *avoid responding to my friend's attempts to contact me*
  when … *my feelings have been hurt by him/her.*
  Instead I will … *initiate a conversation to express how I am feeling in 4 out of 4 opportunities.*

A Past Stressful Situation 28-30
Accomplishment
- I will … *journal about a situation from my past in which I became intensely anxious, by Friday.*

Signs of Stress Symptoms

Take-Away Skills Examples *(Continued)*

Picturing My Stress – NOW and THEN 31
　Accomplishment
　• I will ... *draw a picture of what my stress looks like, to help gain control over it, by Monday.*

Worry-Work and Worry Self-Talk 32-33
　Conditions and Behavior
　• Now, I ... *tell myself that I am a failure*
　　when I ... *receive a lower grade than I expected.*
　　Instead I will ... *allow myself to be mad for 15 minutes and then let it go in 4 out of 4 opportunities.*
　• Now, I ... *avoid going to a party*
　　when I ... *am worried that I will not have anyone to talk to.*
　　Instead I will ... *repeat a positive affirmation to myself and attend the event in 4 out of 4 opportunities.*

Recognizing High Anxiety Situations 34
　Conditions and Behavior
　• Now, I ... *give into peer pressure*
　　when I ... *am asked to drink alcohol even though I don't want to.*
　　Instead I will ... *take a deep breath and say, "No thank you" in 4 out of 4 opportunities.*
　• Now, I ... *clam up and can't speak*
　　when I ... *am put "on the spot" by my teacher.*
　　Instead I will ... *take a deep breath and answer as best I can, in 4 out of 4 opportunities.*

My Anxiety Symptoms 35
　Frequency and Duration
　• I will ... *my physical and emotional symptoms of anxiety in a journal 1 time a day for a week.*

Anxiety Tension 36
　Conditions and Behavior
　• Now, I ... *experience a racing heart and avoid speaking up in class*
　　when I ... *am afraid that other people will laugh at my answer.*
　　Instead I will ... *tell myself "I am smart" and raise my hand in 4 out of 4 opportunities.*

You Have Been Asked 38
　Conditions and Behavior
　• Now, I ... *say "yes" because I am worried that my boyfriend will dump me if I say "no"*
　　when I ... *am asked to go to an event with his family.*
　　Instead I will ... *take a deep breath and then honestly respond, in 4 out of 4 opportunities.*

Basic Anxiety Management Skills 39
　Frequency and Duration
　• I will ... *go for a walk during my lunch break to reduce my anxiety 3 times a week for a month.*
　• I will ... *go to bed at 10:00PM every night for a week.*
　• I will ... *exercise for 30 minutes, 3 times a week for a month.*
　• I will ... *journal my eating habits 1 time a day for a week.*
　• I will ... *do yoga for 15 minutes every day for a month.*

(Continued on next page)

Take-Away Skills Examples *(Continued)*

My Anxiety Symptoms 40
  Frequency and Duration
  - I will … *try out one new relaxation activity once a week for a month.*
  - I will … *take my medications as prescribed once every day for a month.*

  Conditions and Behavior
  - Now, I … *become sick to my stomach*
    when I … *can't stop thinking about a stressor I don't have control over.*
    Instead I will … *distract myself by watching a funny movie, in 4 out of 4 opportunities.*

Quick Meditation 41
  Frequency and Duration
  - I will … *.practice the Quick Meditation exercise to reduce stress 1 time a day for a week.*

Signs of Stress Symptoms Scale
Introduction and Directions

Teens who feel anxious often may experience a wide variety of physical, emotional, and psychological symptoms. A key factor in overcoming their anxiety is to develop the ability to identify signs of stress when they begin to present themselves, and to have knowledge of a few techniques for quickly calming the anxiety.

This assessment contains two scales of twenty statements each, related to how well you recognize the signs of stress that lead to anxiety. Read each of the statements and decide how much the statement describes you.

- If the statement describes you a lot, circle the number under that column next to that item.
- If the statement describes you sometimes, circle the number under that column next to that item.
- If the statement describes you only a little, or not at all, circle the number under that column next to that item.

In the following example, the circled number under "A Lot" indicates the statement is very descriptive a lot of the time of the person completing the assessment.

When I begin to feel stressed, I recognize that…	A Lot	Sometimes	Little/None
I am trembling and shaking	③	2	1

This is not a test. Since there are no right or wrong answers, do not spend too much time thinking about your answers. Be sure to respond to every statement.

(Turn to the next page and begin.)

Signs of Stress Symptoms Scale P

When I begin to feel stressed, I recognize that…	A Lot	Sometimes	Little/None
I am trembling and shaking	3	2	1
My heart is beating faster	3	2	1
I am experiencing intense worry/fear	3	2	1
I am lightheaded or dizzy	3	2	1
I can hardly breathe	3	2	1
I feel very cold	3	2	1
My chest feels tight	3	2	1
My hands are tingly	3	2	1
I have sweaty palms	3	2	1
I feel sick	3	2	1
My hands or feet feel numb	3	2	1
I have sleeping problems	3	2	1
I have headaches	3	2	1
I have muscle tension or aches	3	2	1
I have difficulty swallowing	3	2	1
I have stomach problems and/or nausea	3	2	1
I get dry skin and/or rashes	3	2	1
I use the restroom more often than usual	3	2	1
I become overly tired	3	2	1
I get hot flashes	3	2	1

Scale P = _____

Signs of Stress Symptoms Scale E

When I begin to feel stressed, I recognize that …	A Lot	Sometimes	Little/None
I cry easily and/or often	3	2	1
I cannot control my fears	3	2	1
I am very worried and cannot control it	3	2	1
I don't feel calm in certain situations when I need to	3	2	1
I have fears that may be foolish	3	2	1
I become short-tempered	3	2	1
I get angry easily	3	2	1
I am easily exhausted	3	2	1
I have difficulty concentrating	3	2	1
I feel sad for no reason at all	3	2	1
I am unable to relax	3	2	1
I have irrational thoughts	3	2	1
I avoid situations where I should be present	3	2	1
I avoid people with whom I need to be with	3	2	1
I avoid activities I used to enjoy	3	2	1
I become irritable very easily with others	3	2	1
I have unhappy flashbacks	3	2	1
I have terrible nightmares or bad dreams	3	2	1
I fear losing control	3	2	1
I see everything in a negative way	3	2	1

Scale E = _____

Go to the Scoring Directions

Signs of Stress Symptoms Scales P and E Scoring Directions

Your ability to recognize the signs of stress that lead to anxiety can help you to determine when anxiety is becoming a problem. This will allow you to take action to reduce the feelings of anxiety. This scale is designed to help you explore those signs of stress.

Add the numbers that you circled. Your totals will range from 20 to 60 on each scale.
Then, transfer your totals to the spaces below:

Scale P - Physical Symptoms = _____

Scale E - Emotional Symptoms = _____

Profile Interpretation – Scale P - Physical Symptoms

Place an X on the line below, indicating the score of your physical anxiety symptoms:

20   30   40   50   60

SOME SYMPTOMS   MANY SYMPTOMS

Profile Interpretation – Scale E - Emotional Symptoms

Place an X on the line below, indicating the score of your emotional anxiety symptoms:

20   30   40   50   60

SOME SYMPTOMS   MANY SYMPTOMS

Scale Descriptions

Scale P - Physical Symptoms – Teens scoring High on this scale tend to experience many distressing physical symptoms when they are stressed and become very anxious.

Scale E - Emotional Symptoms – Teens scoring High on this scale tend to experience many distressing emotional symptoms when they are stressed and become very anxious.

Remember that even one symptom, physical or emotional, can be significant in daily functioning!

Signs of Stress Symptoms

Stress in My School Life

Many different sources of stress occur in one's school-life.

Identify some of the situations at school that are currently triggering stress that leads to your anxiety. Place an X in the boxes of the situations that cause you stress and anxiety at or about school. Then write which symptoms you experience when they are happening. If the issue is with one or more person, identify each person with a different name-code (LIC = Likes Ice Cream).

School Issues

- ☐ Boredom _____
- ☐ Being bullied _____
- ☐ Changing teachers _____
- ☐ Change in work to be done _____
- ☐ Experimentation with substances _____
- ☐ Feeling that I'm not good enough _____
- ☐ Frustration _____
- ☐ Gang activity _____
- ☐ Isolation _____
- ☐ Lack of meaning _____
- ☐ Lack of family support _____
- ☐ Loss of good grades _____
- ☐ My expectations are too high _____
- ☐ No appreciation for education _____
- ☐ No control of future _____
- ☐ Not enough hours _____
- ☐ Not valued _____
- ☐ Overloaded _____
- ☐ Peer pressure _____
- ☐ Personal injury _____
- ☐ Physical environment _____
- ☐ Poor health issues _____
- ☐ Poor performance _____
- ☐ Problems at home _____
- ☐ Relationships _____
- ☐ Safety concerns _____
- ☐ Too many extracurricular activities _____
- ☐ Too many hours _____
- ☐ Too much work _____
- ☐ Uncertainty about future _____
- ☐ Unrealistic expectations by parents _____
- ☐ Unequal treatment by teachers _____
- ☐ Unreasonable or unfair expectations by teachers _____
- ☐ Other _____

Being aware of anxiety triggers is the first step in managing them. Now that you have identified the source of stress, who can you talk with that can give to suggestions on how you can reduce the stressors. On the reverse side of this page, write about the stressor that is causing the most anxiety.

Managing Anxiety Workbook for Teens

Stress Associated With My Relationships

Many different sources of stress occur with one's varied relationships.

Identify some of the relationship issues that are currently triggering stress that leads to your anxiety. Place an X in the boxes of the situations that cause you stress and anxiety with any of your relationships. Then write which symptoms you experience when they are happening. If the issue is with one or more person, identify each person by using a name-code (MGF = My Good Friend).

Relationship Issues

☐ Abuse _____
☐ Anger _____
☐ Appreciation _____
☐ Availability _____
☐ Blame _____
☐ Breakup _____
☐ Bullying _____
☐ Compatibility _____
☐ Consistency _____
☐ Control _____
☐ Crisis _____
☐ Death _____
☐ Empathy _____
☐ Expectations _____
☐ Family _____
☐ Finances _____
☐ Getting dumped _____
☐ Growing apart _____
☐ Illness _____
☐ Immaturity _____
☐ Lack of friends _____
☐ Loyalty _____
☐ Peer pressure _____
☐ Respect _____
☐ Sense of security _____
☐ Sex _____
☐ Threats _____
☐ Trust _____
☐ Truthfulness _____
☐ Unclear messages _____
☐ Values _____
☐ Violence _____
☐ Other _____
☐ Other _____

Being aware of anxiety triggers is the first step in managing them. Now that you have identified the source of stress, who can you talk with that can give to suggestions on how you can reduce the stressors. On the reverse side of this page, write about the stressor that is causing the most anxiety.

Signs of Stress Symptoms

My Stress Triggers

It is important to explore the stressful reaction triggers that create anxiety for you.

The following will help you examine what prompts stress in a variety of settings, Place an X in the boxes that apply to you. Then, in the space after each item you check, describe how the item applies to you. The area with the most boxes checked is your greatest source of stress triggers.

At Home
- ☐ When I am asked to do _____
- ☐ When someone _____
- ☐ When I feel like I'm _____
- ☐ When others don't _____
- ☐ When I think _____

At Home TOTAL = _____

At School
- ☐ When I am asked to do _____
- ☐ When someone _____
- ☐ When I feel like I'm _____
- ☐ When others don't _____
- ☐ When I think _____

At School TOTAL = _____

In Social Situations
- ☐ When I am asked to do _____
- ☐ When someone _____
- ☐ When I feel like I'm _____
- ☐ When others don't _____
- ☐ When I think _____

In Social Situations TOTAL = _____

In the Community
- ☐ When I am asked to do _____
- ☐ When someone _____
- ☐ When I feel like I'm _____
- ☐ When others don't _____
- ☐ When I think _____

In the Community TOTAL = _____

A Past Stressful Situation

Think back to a stressful situation that caused you to become intensely anxious. Journaling about that situation can help you better understand the situation and reduce your distress associated with it. **USE NAME CODES.**

In the spaces that follow, journal about your stressful situation.

Describe the situation. _____
_____
_____
_____

How did you get into the situation? _____
_____
_____
_____

Who else plays a role in the situation? _____
_____
_____
_____

What happened? What did you do? _____
_____
_____
_____

What didn't you do? _____
_____
_____
_____

(Continued on the next page)

A Past Stressful Situation *(Continued)*

What, if anything, could have been done differently? _____
_____
_____
_____

What stressed you out the most about the situation? _____
_____
_____
_____

How did you know it was resolved? _____
_____
_____
_____

What did you do after it was over? _____
_____
_____
_____

How have these stressful types of situations changed your life? _____
_____
_____
_____

(Continued on the next page)

A Past Stressful Situation (Continued)

How has it affected your present life? _____

_____

_____

_____

How has the event affected your future life? _____

_____

_____

_____

What was the worst aspect of the situation? _____

_____

_____

_____

Did you resolve your stress issue? _____ If not, how can you resolve your stress issue? _____

_____

_____

_____

What is something positive that has come out of the event? *(example: relationships, new job, wisdom)*

_____

_____

_____

_____

_____

Signs of Stress Symptoms

Picturing My Stress – NOW and THEN

We all have stress, and stress leads to anxiety. When that anxiety becomes intense, we need to be able to manage it.

One way to begin to gain control over stress and/or panic is to use your imagination, visualize what your stress looks or feels like, and draw a picture or a caricature of it.

What My Stress and Stressor(s) Look Like NOW

My Stress Looks Like	The Cause(s) of My Stress Looks Like

What I Would Like My Stress and Stressor(s) to Look Like

My Stress Looks Like	The Cause(s) of My Stress Looks Like

Worry-Work

Many people who experience intense anxiety tend to focus on the negatives in their lives. These negatives are often contained in the continuous running tape in their heads (self-talk).

In detail, describe the negative things you most often say to yourself, and then list the positives you could say instead. If you need more space, use a blank sheet of paper.
If you are going to refer to another person, use a name code. (MAS = My Aunt Susie)

My Greatest Worry_____

Negative things I Say to Myself
   Example:
   I will never get into college with my grades.

Positive Things I Could Say to Myself
   I will do everything in my power to raise my grade point average, but I will not obsess about it.

Signs of Stress Symptoms

Worry Self-Talk

The conversations that go on in your head can cause you tremendous amounts of anxiety.

Answer the following questions to explore your type of negative self-talk you. Circle the 3, 2, or 1 for each item (be honest!) and then add your scores to get your totals.

	True	Sometimes True	NOT True
I worry all the time	3	2	1
I imagine the worst thing that can happen	3	2	1
I worry about what might happen	3	2	1
I worry about being embarrassed	3	2	1
I anticipate the worst	3	2	1

Worry Wart Scale = _____

I judge myself	3	2	1
I evaluate my behavior harshly	3	2	1
I focus on my mistakes	3	2	1
I always compare myself with others	3	2	1
I overlook my positive qualities and focus on the negatives	3	2	1

Critic Scale = _____

I believe I'm not doing enough	3	2	1
I feel like I should be working harder	3	2	1
I hate when I make a mistake	3	2	1
I don't have goals for the future	3	2	1
I usually say "I should have _____"	3	2	1

Perfectionist Scale = _____

The Scales on which you scored high, indicates the type of negative self-talk that happens in your head and heightens your anxiety. Transfer your totals below The Range is 5 (not at all) to 15 (a lot!)

Worry Wart _____   Critic _____   Perfectionist _____

What are your observations about the results? _____

_____

Recognizing High Anxiety Situations

It is important to be aware of and identify your high-anxiety situations; to attempt to avoid them, and if you can't, be prepared to deal with the stress that will arise. **Use Name Codes.**

What are your high-anxiety situations and how can you cope with them more effectively?

My High-Anxiety Situations	When I Encounter this Situation	How I React	How I Can Cope
Example: When a person with whom I want as a friend asks me to go out drinking.	Often after school.	I get sweaty and begin to feel dizzy..	I will take deep breaths and assertively say "No thanks, not interested."

Which high-anxiety situations are particularly worrisome to you? _____

_____

_____

What steps can you take immediately to either avoid them or feel less stressed in that situation?

_____

_____

Signs of Stress Symptoms

My Anxiety Symptoms

Anxiety symptoms can be both physical and emotional. Which do you have most?

Take time to explore your anxiety symptoms, where they occur and what makes them better or worse. USE NAME CODES.

Symptoms	Where They Occur	What Makes Them Worse	What Makes Them Better
Example: My heart beats very fast, and then I can hardly breathe.	At school during lunch, when the class bullies are around.	When I try to hide and look invisible.	It gets better if I take several deep breaths. I need to tell someone I trust about my fears.

If you don't think your anxiety, depression, sadness, and stress impacts your physical health, think again.

~ Kris Carr

What does the above quotation say to you and why is it important? _____
_____
_____

Anxiety Tension

Teens who have an intense level of anxiety are often unable to recognize tension and how they experience it. **This handout will help you explore how you experience tension when you are anxious. USE NAME CODES.**

External events leading to feelings of anxiety	Where in my body I feel the tension	Internal negative thoughts leading to feelings of anxiety	Internal positive thoughts leading to lessen feelings of anxiety
Example: Speaking in front of my peers.	I get an upset stomach and get light-headed.	Some people will make fun of me.	Certain people are just that way. I can live with it!

What is one thing can you do to eliminate or reduce your feelings of anxiety? _____

_____

_____

_____

Signs of Stress Symptoms

Effects of Anxiety

Awareness of the effects of anxiety is the first step in overcoming it. It is important for you to think about the various ways that you feel because of your anxiety.

How does anxiety affect your day-to-day activities and interactions? USE NAME CODES.

Setting	When I Become Anxious	How It Affects Me	How It Affects Others
Example: People	I become anxious when I'm at a party where there are drugs.	I get jittery and can't sit still.	They think I'm strange.
People			
School			
Home			
Friends			
Other			

You Have Been Asked …

It is important to recognize the thoughts, feelings and emotions that accompany your stress that eventually lead to anxiety. One of the best ways to do this is to identify a situation and then practice letting go of the thoughts, emotions, and behaviors associated with this situation.

Write about something that you have been asked to do that always seems to stress you out, heighten your anxiety, and/or panic you. _____

_____
_____
_____

Take a deep breath … and … respond.

Notice any thoughts about your above comments and write them. _____

_____
_____
_____

Let them go.

Notice any emotions about your above comments and write them. _____

_____
_____
_____

Let them go.

Notice any emotions about your above comments and write them. _____

_____
_____
_____

Let them go.

Signs of Stress Symptoms

Basic Anxiety Management Tools

Below, journal about lifestyle changes you can make to help reduce your anxiety.

EXERCISE REGULARLY: Attempt to get at least 30 minutes or more of aerobic activity each day.

My Exercise Habits _____

_____

_____

How I Can Do Better _____

_____

HEALTHY EATING HABITS: Eat plenty of complex carbohydrates such as whole grains, fruits, and vegetables. Limit sugars and omit alcohol.

My Eating Habits _____

_____

_____

How I Can Do Better _____

_____

SLEEP: Get enough sleep to maintain your emotional balance and reduce anxiety.

My Sleep Habits _____

_____

_____

How I Can Do Better _____

_____

RELAXATION: Engage in techniques that will relax you including yoga, meditation, and deep breathing.

My Relaxation Habits _____

_____

_____

How I Can Do Better _____

_____

Managing Anxiety Workbook for Teens

My Coping Strategies

It is important that you learn basic techniques for coping with and managing your stress. By doing so, you will reduce the amounts of anxiety that you experience.

Think back over the past week, and describe which types of coping mechanisms you used, how effective they were, and the end results. Complete this table in the second, third, or fourth column to identify effective stress-management techniques.

Techniques	I Tried and Liked It. Why I Like It.	I Have Not Tried It. Why I Haven't.	I Tried and Do Not Like it. Why Not.
Example: *Relaxation.*	*When I feel stress, I immediately put in my ear buds and listen to my favorite music. I like it because it is always with me and easy to do.*		
Relaxation – *Find a quiet place to relax, meditate, do yoga, listen to soothing music, draw, use a guided imagery CD, write, color.*			
Breathing – *Take time to just breathe. Take deep breaths in through your nose and breathe out through your mouth.*			
Prescribed Meds – *Be sure that you have taken your medications as prescribed by a physician.*			
Support – *Confide in and talk with trusted friends and family and/ or therapist about your stress and anxiety.*			
Distract Myself – *Find productive, relaxing, and enjoyable ways, to take your mind off your anxiety.*			
Other			

Signs of Stress Symptoms

Quick Meditation

When you begin to experience signs of stress and start to feel anxious, it can be very helpful to do a quick meditation to reduce the stress quickly and easily. Meditation is easy and helps you relax, become calm, and stop the thoughts about the event from flooding back into your consciousness.

Here is the *Quick Meditation* process:

1. Right now, think of a place that is calming to you, such as a clearing in a forest, a prime spot on a beach, a balcony on a cruise, etc.

2. With this image in your mind, gently close your eyes and focus on this image. If you have thoughts (other than those that belong in your calm place), acknowledge them and let them go.

3. After one minute, open your eyes.

How do you feel right now? _____

_____

_____

What thoughts popped back into your head? _____

_____

_____

How does your stress feel now? _____

_____

_____

How does your anxiety feel now? _____

_____

_____

**Keep practicing this daily for five to ten minutes,
and you will notice your anxiety becoming less prominent.**

MY KRYPTONITE

Superman could do just about anything and was not afraid of anything. However, even Superman had his kryptonite. For Superman, kryptonite was a mineral from the planet Krypton that drained Superman of his strength. He was not able to overcome it – he avoided it. Can you overcome it?

On the minerals below, write about various aspects of your kryptonite, or those things that take your strength away and fill you with anxiety. For example, if you are afraid to speak in public, you might write about fear of how people will evaluate you, how you might embarrass yourself, others laughing at you, etc.

My kryptonite is …

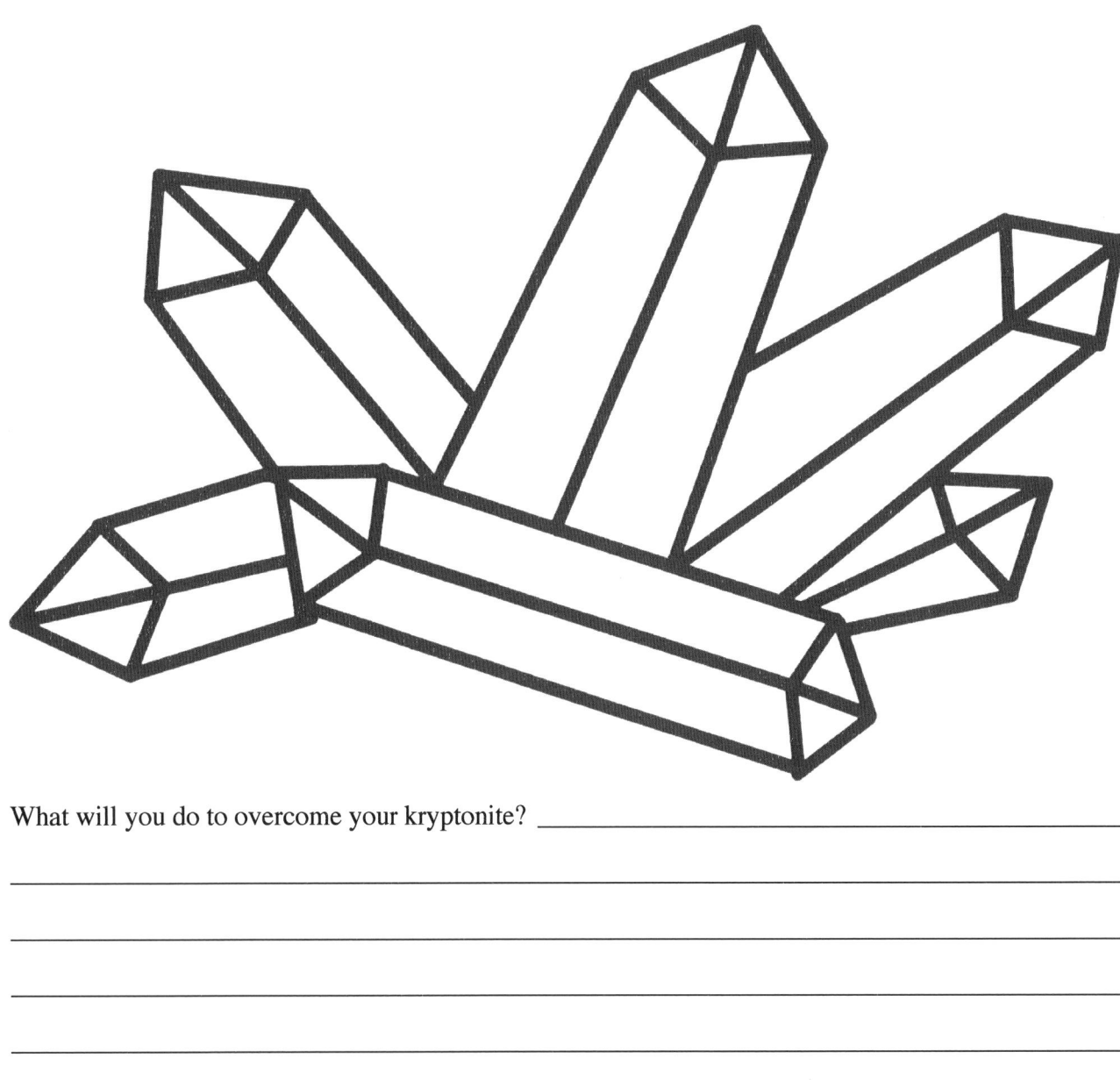

What will you do to overcome your kryptonite? _____

_____

_____

_____

_____

MODULE II

Need for Control

*Grant me the serenity …
to accept the people I cannot
change, the courage to
change the one I can, and
the wisdom to know it's me.*

~ ***Adaptation of The Serenity Prayer***

Name _____

Date _____

Module II – Take-Away Skills

We have included skills for most of the handouts in each Module, *Conditions and Behavior* (1), *Frequency and Duration* (2), and/or *Accomplishment* (3) statements for each activity may be used in educational and/or treatment planning, and also used to measure progress toward goals. These Take-Away skills promote real life outcomes and behavioral changes. Feel free to add additional skills for each activity.

Examples

1. **Conditions and Behavior** – a skill or healthy habit to replace a previous less effective behavior/habit.
   - Now, I … *(less effective or undesired behavior)*
     when I … *(when do I do this?)*.
     Instead I will … *(more effective or desired new behavior)* in ___ out of ___ opportunities.
2. **Frequency and Duration** – a skill or healthy habit not necessarily tied to a condition or previous behavior.
   - I will *(describe the behavior)* _____ times per _____.
3. **Accomplishment** – an outcome that is a one-time accomplishment.
   - I will *(describe the accomplishment)* by _____ *(date)*.

Take-Away Skills Examples

Control or Not? 50
Conditions and Behavior
- Now, I … *become angry*
  when … *my parents impose a curfew that I don't think is fair.*
  Instead I will … *respect my parents' rules and prove that I can be trusted in 4 out of 4 opportunities.*
- Now, I … *worry that something bad has happened to my friends*
  when … *they don't text me back right away.*
  Instead I will … *stop and determine if my worry is rational or irrational, in 4 out of 4 opportunities.*

Changes in My Life 51
Conditions and Behavior
- Now, I … *isolate from others*
  when I … *am going through a break-up.*
  Instead I will … *talk to a close confidante for support in 4 out of 4 opportunities.*

My IF Fears 52
Conditions and Behavior
- Now, I … *don't ask for what I want*
- when I … *am afraid that the answer will be "no.*
  Instead I will … *remind myself that I will never get what I want if I don't ask in 4 out of 4 opportunities.*

Need for Control

Take-Away Skills Examples *(Continued)*

Doodling 54
Accomplishment
- I will … *create a doodle representing my future, by the end of the week.*

Taking Action to Reduce Anxiety 55
Accomplishment
- I will … *set one long-term goal for my future by the end of the week.*
- I will … *identify three short-term goals as steps toward reaching my long-term goal, by the March 31st.*
- I will … *join a sports team to help achieve my goal of making new friends, by the end of the month.*

Frequency and Duration
- I will … *complete one short-term goal off of my list, 1 time every week for 1 month.*

Over and Over and Over Again! 56
Conditions and Behavior
- Now, I … *keep telling tell myself that I am a failure*
  when I … *do poorly on a test.*
  Instead I will … *stop my thought and recognize that just because I've had one bad test does not make me a failure in 4 out of 4 opportunities.*

What's the Worst Thing? 58
Conditions and Behavior
- Now, I … *worry excessively*
  when I … *think about having to do a presentation in class.*
  Instead I will … *think about the worst thing that could happen to reduce my anxiety in 4 out of 4 opportunities.*

From a Self-Fulfilling Prophecy to Imagining the Best 59
Conditions and Behavior
- Now, I … *avoid going to a school club meeting*
  when I … *don't think I will not know anyone.*
  Instead I will … *think about all of the good things that could happen there, in 4 out of 4 opportunities.*

Staying in the Present 60
Conditions and Behavior
- Now, I … *experience my mind wandering*
  when I … *think about all of the things that could go wrong in my relationship.*
  Instead I will … *bring my attention back to the word "peace" in 4 out of 4 opportunities.*

Frequency and Duration
- I will … *engage in 15 minutes of mindful meditation one time a day for a week.*

Deep Breathing and Relaxing Your Body 61- 62
Frequency and Duration
- I will … *complete a Body Scan deep breathing exercise 1 time a day for 2 weeks.*
- I will … *practice Total-Body Relaxation 1 time a day for a week.*

Mindfulness and Mindfulness Journaling 63- 64
Frequency and Duration
- I will … *practice a mindfulness exercise for 15 minutes 1 time a day for 1 week.*
- I will … *journal about the mindfulness exercise after practicing it 1 time a day for a week.*

Managing Anxiety Workbook for Teens

Need for Control Scale
Introduction and Directions

The need for control is often a reaction to the fear of losing control. People who feel the need for control are typically afraid of being in unpredictable situations, feeling vulnerable, and/or living with uncertainty. They often feel a strong need for control and become very anxious when control eludes them.

This assessment contains 18 statements designed to help you explore the ways in which you become anxious because of the need to feel in control. Read each of the statements and decide whether the statement describes you or not. If the statement does describe you, circle the number in the YES column next to that item. If the statement does not describe you, circle the number in the NO column next to that item. Do not worry about the numbers for now.

In the following example, the circled 2 indicates the statement does not describe the person completing the inventory:

		YES	NO
1.	I feel a need to be in control at all times	1	(2)

This is not a test. Since there are no right or wrong answers, do not spend too much time thinking about your answers. Be sure to respond to every statement.

(Turn to the next page and begin.)

Need for Control Scale

	YES	NO
1. I feel a need to be in control at all times	2	1
2. I worry about what others teens think of me	2	1
3. I want to control everything that happens to me	2	1
4. It's hard for me to trust that anyone else will do things correctly	2	1
5. I often feel powerless and don't like it	2	1
6. I don't like feeling helpless	2	1

Scale V = _____

7. I worry about bad things that are happening in the world	2	1
8. I worry about being in new situations	2	1
9. I lack self-confidence around people I don't know	2	1
10. I worry about making the wrong decisions	2	1
11. I worry in situations in which I have no control	2	1
12. I worry when some things change that I can't control	2	1

Scale S = _____

13. I worry about the unknown	2	1
14. I usually imagine the worst	2	1
15. I need to feel in control to feel safe	2	1
16. I worry when I don't know what's going to happen	2	1
17. I worry about the future	2	1
18. I worry about unfamiliar situations	2	1

Scale U = _____

Go to the Scoring Directions

Need for Control Scale
Scoring Directions

The *Need for Control Scale* you just completed is designed to measure how a lack of control bothers you. For each of the sections on the previous page, count the scores you circled. Put that total on the line marked TOTAL at the end of each section.

Then, transfer your total to the space below:

      V Vulnerable Total   = _____

      S Situational Total   = _____

      U Uncertainty Total   = _____

Add your scores together for your Grand Total.   _____

Profile Interpretation

Individual Score	Grand Total	Result	Indications
6 – 7	18 – 23	Low	Low scores indicate that you are not experiencing much anxiety due to the need for control. Complete the following exercises to continue.
8 – 10	24 – 30	Moderate	Moderate scores indicate that you are experiencing some anxiety due to the need for control. Complete the following exercises to continue.
11 – 12	31 – 36	High	High scores indicate that you are experiencing a great deal of anxiety due to the need for control. Complete the following exercises to continue.

Scale Descriptions

Vulnerable – Teens scoring High on this scale become anxious because they do not always trust others, need to be in control of their environment, and hate to feel vulnerable and powerless.

Situational – Teens scoring High on this scale do not like to experience change; they become anxious when confronted with new situations, and they worry about problems occurring in the world.

Uncertainty – Teens scoring High on this scale tend to worry about the unknown, and about the future. They do not feel safe if they are not in complete control of their lives.

GRAND TOTAL – High scores on all three scales indicate that the teen tends to become very anxious and full of worry when not feeling in control of their lives or their environment. They do not like to feel vulnerable or powerless, they dislike facing new situations, and they constantly worry about the future.

Control or Not?

It is important to examine the areas in your life that you can control and those you cannot control. **Identify what you cannot control and what you can control in the various areas in your life. USE NAME CODES.**

Areas of My Life	What I Cannot Control	What I Can Control
Example: At Home.	I cannot control my parents' curfew for me.	I can control my behavior. If I prove I can be trusted, they might change the curfew..
At Home		
In School		
In the Community		
In My Personal Life		
In My Social Life		
At Work / Volunteer		
Other		

In which areas of your life do you have the ability to control? _____

_____

_____

How can you let go of the things you cannot control? _____

_____

_____

Need for Control

Changes in My Life

Change is anxiety-producing for some people. Change is stepping into the unknown and can increase the amounts of stress and anxiety experienced. What is changing in your life?

Write about these changes and explore how your perceptions affect your feelings about the change. USE NAME CODES.

A Change In My Life	Is This Change in My Control? Why or why not?	Is This Change Comfortable for Me? Why?	Is This Change Uncomfortable for Me? Why?	How I Can Look at This Change in a Positive Light
Example: A breakup.	No. She wanted to date someone else.	I don't think we had that much in common anyway.	Yes – I will see her in math class & probably wish we were together.	I can start dating another person I like.

Why is the unknown so scary? _____

_____

_____

My "IF" Fears

Fears are often triggered because of a lack of control over one's environment. One wonders, *What if this happens?* or *What if that happens?* Fears can be rational or irrational.
What are your "IF" fears? How are they interfering with your ability to lead a satisfying life?

In the spaces that follow, list your fears and how they are related to a lack of control. USE NAME CODES.

My "IF" Fears	Rational or Irrational	How They are Tied to a Lack of Control	What I Can Do To Overcome These Fears
Example: IF I don't get into the college I want it will be terrible.	Irrational	I cannot control the admissions office.	I can have other colleges on my list!

Need for Control

Go to Your Fears

> *Go to your fears, sit with them, stare at them. Your fears are your friend; their only job is to show you undeveloped parts of yourself that you need to cultivate to live a happy life. The more you do the things you're most afraid of doing, the more life opens up. Embrace your fears and they will embrace you.*
>
> **~ Jackson Kiddard**

What does this quotation say to you? _____
_____
_____
_____
_____

What are your fears? _____
_____
_____
_____
_____

When have you done things you were afraid of doing? _____
_____
_____
_____
_____

How did it work out, and how could it have worked out differently? _____
_____
_____
_____
_____

Which fear are you ready to embrace? _____
_____
_____
_____
_____

Doodling

Doodling is an excellent way for you to unleash the power of self-expression.

You do not need to be an artist to doodle. You are the only one who needs to know what the doodle represents. Doodling is simply drawing something without worrying about how it will look to other people. It is designed to help you put your left brain (your logical brain) on hold while you use your right brain (the creative part of your brain). Doodles can be silly designs, drawings, icons, abstract shapes, lines, or intermittent words to represent your personal thoughts.

I wish I had more control over …	**Weakness looks like …**

Uncertainty looks like …	**The future looks like …**

Need for Control

Taking Action to Reduce Anxiety

> *Nothing diminishes anxiety faster than action.*
> *~ Walter Anderson*

What is a long-term action goal that will help you to feel less anxious about the future? Write that long-term action goal below. Then, in the table below, set several smaller goals to achieve this long-term goal. Be as specific as you possibly can be.

My Long-Term Goal: _____

_____

My Short-Term Goals in Order to Reach My Long Term-Goal	What I Can do To Achieve This Short-Term Goal	How It Will Contribute to My Long-Term Goal
1.		
2.		
3.		
4.		
5.		

If you have more than 5 short term goals, continue on the back of the page.

Managing Anxiety Workbook for Teens

Over and Over and Over Again!

Often, people who are very anxious have thoughts, images, or impulses that occur over and over again, and things that feel outside of their control. They are usually intense and uncomfortable.

Write about them below. USE NAME CODES.

Situation	Thoughts, Images, and Impulses that Repeat Over and Over Again	How These Thoughts, Images and Impulses Affect Me
Example: Every time I have to take a final test I get physically ill.	I'll never get into college. My parents will be furious and make my life miserable.	I don't sleep well the night before. In the morning I break out in a rash and my hands are so sweaty I can barely hold a pencil.

If you need more space, please use the reverse side of this handout.

Need for Control

Hocus-Focus

If you need more space, please use the reverse side of this handout.

People with intense anxiety often have repeating thoughts that keep them focused on their anxious thoughts rather than actions to reduce the anxiety.

Below are a set of magical steps that you can take to dramatically reduce your feelings of anxiety by focusing on your behaviors and not your thoughts.

Describe a situation in which you had obtrusive, repeating thoughts: _____

_____

_____

In the space next to each magic wand below, write how you could refocus your attention.

Step 1: Recognize and re-label intrusive thoughts that tell you that something is wrong:

Step 2: Focus your attention on something else:

Step 3: Pay attention and focus on your next behaviors and not on your thoughts:

What's the Worst Thing?

When you are worrying, try asking yourself, What's the worst thing that can happen? Often people find out that the worst thing isn't really that bad, and often the worst thing doesn't happen!

Think about a time lately when you felt anxious about something that might happen in the future.

What was the situation? _____
_____
_____
_____

When you think about it, what emotions did you experience? _____
_____
_____
_____

How did you experience the anxiety in your body? _____
_____
_____
_____

What was the worst thing that could have happened in this situation? _____
_____
_____
_____

What did happen? _____
_____
_____
_____

In the future, ask yourself these questions and focus on the positive? It IS POSSIBLE that it will turn out okay. Staying positive helps! _____
_____
_____
_____

From a Self-Fulfilling Prophecy to Imagining the Best

When you focus on everything that can go wrong, you are putting into motion a self-fulfilling prophecy for yourself. In other words, when you imagine how something in the future will be bad or go wrong, it possibly will! For this activity, let's turn that around.

Think about an event that you have coming up in the future and write about all of the good things that will happen at this event. Be creative!

Event: _____

_____

_____

_____

_____

Good things that can happen (be specific): _____

_____

_____

_____

_____

Steps you need to take to make sure good things will happen (be specific): _____

_____

_____

_____

_____

Now LET GO of the negative thinking. How can you do that? _____

_____

_____

_____

_____

Staying in the Present

Paying attention and attending to whatever you are doing in the present is one of the best ways to reduce anxiety related to the unknown future. Being attentive can lessen the impact and help you to step back from thoughts and feelings about the future or the past.

Let's practice mindfulness now.
1. Look around you and focus on something of interest to you.
2. Concentrate on the object.
3. Each time your mind begins to wander from the object, bring it back to full attention.
4. Do this for several minutes.
5. Then journal about the following questions.

How did you feel during that mindfulness activity? _____
_____
_____

Did you have difficulty attending to the object? If so, why? _____
_____
_____
_____

What did you notice about your thoughts as you mindfully attended to the object? _____
_____
_____
_____

How can this help you? _____
_____
_____
_____

Deep Breathing

> *When you own your breath, nobody can steal your peace.*
> ~ **Author Unknown**

Deep breathing can help reduce your anxiety the following ways:
- Reduces hyperventilation when you encounter stressors
- Helps you feel calm
- Helps you reduce anxiety quickly
- Reduces everyday stress
- Reduce panic and anxiety

1. Scan your body and identify the parts of your body where you are experiencing your anxiety. List those parts of your body: _____
   _____
   _____

2. Next, inhale slowly through your nose until you see your abdomen rising. Hold this breath for five seconds.

3. Then, exhale through your mouth slowly, pushing all of the air out. Do this again five times until you feel more relaxed.

How can you use this technique when you are feeling anxious? _____
_____
_____
_____

How do you think this technique might help you? _____
_____
_____
_____

How do you think this technique would not help you? _____
_____
_____
_____

Relaxing Your Body

Anxiety manifests itself through physical symptoms in your body. These physical symptoms often reinforce your anxiety-producing thoughts and feelings. Total-Body Relaxation (often called Progressive Muscle Relaxation) is a simple technique used to stop anxiety by relaxing all of the muscles throughout your body one group at a time.

Read through the following script several times before you attempt to do this exercise.

1. *Take a few deep breaths, and begin to relax.*
2. *Get comfortable and put aside all of your worries.*
3. *Let each part of your body begin to relax ... starting with your feet.*
4. *Imagine your feet relaxing as all of your tension begins to fade away.*
5. *Imagine the relaxation moving up into your calves and thighs ... feel them beginning to relax.*
6. *Allow the relaxation to move into your waist.*
7. *Continue now to let the relaxation move into your hips and stomach.*
8. *Your entire body from the waist down is now completely relaxed.*
9. *Let go of any strain and discomfort you might feel.*
10. *Allow the relaxation to move into your chest until your chest feels completely relaxed.*
11. *Just enjoy the feeling of complete relaxation.*
12. *Continue to let the relaxation move through the muscles of your shoulders, then spread down into your upper arms, into your elbows, and finally all the way down to your wrists and hands.*
13. *Put aside all of your worries.*
14. *Let yourself be totally present in the moment and let yourself relax more and more. Let all the muscles in your neck unwind and let the relaxation move into your chin and jaws.*
15. *Feel the tension around your eyes flow away as the relaxation moves throughout your face and head.*
16. *Feel your forehead relax and your entire head beginning to feel lighter.*
17. *Let yourself drift deeper and deeper into relaxation and peace.*

After you have read the above paragraph several times, find a quiet location where you can practice Total-Body Relaxation.

- Assume a comfortable position in a chair.
- Take off your jewelry and glasses so that you are totally free.
- Try to let the relaxation happen without having to force it.
- If during the relaxation you lose concentration, don't be concerned - just begin again.

Need for Control

Mindfulness

Mindfulness can help you to live in the moment and worry less about the unknowns. Teens who feel like they need control can experience that feeling by being mindful of the present and accepting it without judgment.

Try these activities to help develop mindfulness. Journal about your experience.

Mindfulness Meditation – For this activity, sit quietly and focus on your natural breathing movements. Now begin to focus on the word peacefulness and repeat it silently to yourself with each breath. Allow thoughts to come and go by simply returning to focus on the word peacefulness. Do this for about two minutes. What was this experience like for you? _____

_____

_____

_____

_____

_____

_____

Body Mindfulness – For this activity, sit quietly and focus on your subtle bodily changes (eye twitching, foot tingling, etc.). Scan your body from head to toe, noting any sensations. Dismiss any thoughts, acknowledge any sensations, and then return to your scanning. Do this for two minutes. What was this experience like for you? _____

_____

_____

_____

_____

_____

_____

Which did you like best and why? _____

_____

Mindfulness Journaling

Mindfulness is being aware of the present moment and not allowing yourself to be pulled into the past or the future.

Complete the activity and then journal about your results. USE NAME CODES.

Take a minute right now to focus all of your attention on your breathing. Keep your eyes open and just breathe normally. Be aware of when your mind begins to wander and return your attention to your breath when this happens. Journal about your experience below:

How difficult was it to keep your mind on your breathing? _____
_____
_____
_____

What did you find your mind doing? _____
_____
_____
_____

What thoughts did you have about the past? _____
_____
_____
_____

What thoughts did you have about the future? _____
_____
_____
_____

Use this exercise during the day to bring your attention back to the present to restore peace and calm.

MODULE III

Social Approval

Most fears of rejection rest on the desire for approval from other people. Don't base your self-esteem on their opinions.

~ Harvey Mackay

Name _____

Date _____

Managing Anxiety Workbook for Teens

Module III – Take-Away Skills

We have included skills for most of the handouts in each Module, *Conditions and Behavior* (1), *Frequency and Duration* (2), and/or *Accomplishment* (3) statements for each activity may be used in educational and/or treatment planning, and also used to measure progress toward goals. These Take-Away skills promote real life outcomes and behavioral changes. Feel free to add additional skills for each activity.

Examples

1. **Conditions and Behavior** – a skill or healthy habit to replace a previous less effective behavior/habit.
   - Now, I … *(less effective or undesired behavior)*
     when I … *(when do I do this?)*.
     Instead I will … *(more effective or desired new behavior)* in ___ out of ___ opportunities.
2. **Frequency and Duration** – a skill or healthy habit not necessarily tied to a condition or previous behavior.
   - I will *(describe the behavior)* _____ times per _____.
3. **Accomplishment** – an outcome that is a one-time accomplishment.
   - I will *(describe the accomplishment)* by _____ *(date)*.

Take-Away Skills Examples

Events Where I Feel Anxious 71
Conditions and Behavior
- Now, I … *avoid going to the cafeteria*
  when … *my best friend is absent from school*.
  Instead I will … *go to the cafeteria at lunchtime, regardless of whether or not my friend is with me, in 5 out of 5 opportunities*.
- Now, I … *say "no" out of fear of doing something that will embarrass me*
  when … *someone asks me to go to a party*.
  Instead I will … *tell myself a positive affirmation and say "yes" in 3 out of 4 opportunities*.

People with Whom I Feel Anxious 72
Conditions and Behavior
- Now, I … *avoid going to youth group*
  when I … *know my ex-girlfriend will be there*.
  Instead I will … *attend youth group to get my spiritual needs met, regardless of whether or not my ex-girlfriend is there, in 5 out of 5 opportunities*.

Situations in Which I Feel Anxious 73
Accomplishment
- I will … *write down all of the situations I've avoided during the week because to my anxiety, and what I miss by avoiding the situation, 1 time a week for a month*.

Take-Away Skills Examples *(Continued)*

Ways I Avoid Social Situations..**74**
Conditions and Behavior
- Now, I ... *drink alcohol to increase my social comfort*
  when I ... *am at a party.*
  Instead I will ... *remind myself of the consequences of this behavior in 4 out of 4 opportunities.*

Need for Approval..**76**
Conditions and Behavior
- Now, I ... *go along with whatever my friends want*
  when I ... *worry that they will not agree with me.*
  Instead I will ... *express my opinion to my friends in 4 out of 4 times.*
- Now, I ... *avoid asking questions*
  when I ... *am afraid my peers will think I am stupid.*
  Instead I will ... *ask for clarification when I do not understand, in 4 out of 4 opportunities.*

I'm Good Enough..**78**
Conditions and Behavior
- Now, I ... *"tense up"*
  when I ... *think someone is looking at and judging me.*
  Instead I will ... *use deep breathing to remain calm, in 4 out of 4 opportunities.*

Challenging Negative Thinking..**80**
Conditions and Behavior
- Now, I ... *automatically say "no" out of fear*
  when ... *someone asks me out on a date.*
  Instead I will ... *stop and determine if it is my anxiety 'talking' before making a decision, in 4 out of 4 opportunities.*

Ways Thinking Can Be Debilitating..**81**
Conditions and Behavior
- Now, I ... *become humiliated*
  when ... *my voice shakes during a presentation.*
  Instead I will ... *tell myself I did the best I could and move on in 4 out of 4 opportunities.*

Positive Self-Talk Scripts..**82**
Conditions and Behavior
- Now, I ... *think about the worst-case scenario*
  when I ... *want to join a new club.*
  Instead I will ... *stop and rehearse a positive self-talk script, in 4 out of 4 opportunities.*

Meet New People..**83**
Frequency and Duration
- I will ... *try out a different after-school club 1 times every month for 3 months.*
- I will ... *volunteer at the local animal shelter 1 time a week for 1 month.*

Self-Appreciation..**84**
Accomplishment
- I will ... *create a collage highlighting what I appreciate about myself by next Friday.*

Social Approval

Social Situation and Social Perception Scale
Introduction and Directions

Many people get anxious and/or self-conscious on occasions, for instance, when speaking up in class, going for a job interview, or having a first date. However, social anxiety is more than shyness or occasional anxiousness. Teens who have social concerns and/or experience social anxiety often worry about being the center of attention, scrutinized, judged, disliked, and/or evaluated negatively.

They feel the need for having social approval, especially when they have fears of certain social situations which are unfamiliar to them or when they feel they are being watched or evaluated by others. They fear saying or doing something embarrassing or making mistakes, and become anxious just thinking about them. They may go to great lengths to avoid these situations

The Social Situation Scale and the Social Perception Scale each contain 22 statements designed to help you explore the level of how much you need social approval and the degree to which a lack of social approval creates anxiety for you. Read each of the statements and decide whether the statement describes you or not, in ways you react in social situations.

If the statement does describe you, circle the number in the YES column next to that item.
If the statement does not describe you, circle the number in the NO column next to that item.

In the following examples, the circled YES indicates the statement describes the person completing the scale:

SOCIAL SITUATION SCALE

In social situations ...

I worry for weeks ahead when I have to speak aloud in class	**YES**	NO

SOCIAL PERCEPTION SCALE

In social situations ...

I believe that I always mess up	**YES**	NO

This is not a test. Since there are no right or wrong answers, do not spend too much time thinking about your answers. Be sure to respond to every statement.

(Turn to the next page and begin.)

Social Situation Scale

In social situations …

I worry for weeks ahead when I have to speak aloud in class	YES	NO
I avoid large groups	YES	NO
I become very nervous when I am involved in a social situation	YES	NO
I don't like meeting people I don't know	YES	NO
I feel awful if I handle a social situation poorly	YES	NO
I have no idea of how to make small talk	YES	NO
I use a substance before I go into a setting with other people	YES	NO
I insist on having a friend come with me in a new social situation	YES	NO
I blush and then get more embarrassed	YES	NO
I avoid being with people I don't know well	YES	NO
I hate when I am the center of attention	YES	NO
I don't like using public bathrooms	YES	NO
I sometimes pretend I am sick when I need to do something socially	YES	NO
I am very self-conscious when I am with anyone I don't know well	YES	NO
I feel anxious if anyone watches me doing anything	YES	NO
I never volunteer to say anything in class	YES	NO
I avoid parties because I don't feel as if I fit in	YES	NO
I am more anxious on a phone call than I am with a text or email	YES	NO
I am self-conscious eating in front of other people	YES	NO
I cannot perform in front of other people even though I have the talent	YES	NO
I choke up when trying to say something when I meet a new person	YES	NO
I stay in the background to avoid being noticed	YES	NO

SOCIAL SITUATION TOTAL = _____

Social Approval

Social Perception Scale

In social situations …

I believe that I always mess up	YES	NO
I believe that the opinions of others are more important than mine	YES	NO
I believe I am concerned about looking foolish to others	YES	NO
I believe I am inferior to others who are smarter than I am	YES	NO
I believe feedback is always hurtful	YES	NO
I believe I will be laughed at for expressing different opinions	YES	NO
I believe people think I am ignorant when their opinions are contrary to mine	YES	NO
I believe that I will become tense if someone is looking my way	YES	NO
I believe people have unfavorable first impressions of me	YES	NO
I believe that people think I blow things out of proportion	YES	NO
I believe that I react poorly when I think someone disapproves of me	YES	NO
I believe that everyone finds fault with my actions	YES	NO
I believe that when I say something aloud, I will feel embarrassed	YES	NO
I believe that I am always being judged by others	YES	NO
I believe that I spend too much time worrying about how others perceive me	YES	NO
I believe I did something wrong when people of authority are around me	YES	NO
I believe that I will be laughed at by others when I do or say something	YES	NO
I believe when I apply for a job I will appear too anxious	YES	NO
I believe that I am a wreck before a first date and then act like it	YES	NO
I believe that my voice will tremble if I talk and people will notice it	YES	NO
I believe that I will usually humiliate myself	YES	NO
I believe that others judge me and it bothers me	YES	NO

SOCIAL PERCEPTION TOTAL = _____

Social Situation and Social Perception Scale Scoring Directions

The *Social Situation and Social Perception Scales* you just completed are designed to measure your need of social approval from others in social situations and how anxious you are about how you are perceived by others. **Count the YES words you circled on the previous pages.** Put that total on the line marked **TOTAL** at the end of each scale and transfer it below. Then add your two scores for your **GRAND TOTAL**.

Social Situation Scale = _____

Social Perception Scale = _____

GRAND TOTAL = _____

Profile Interpretation

Total	Grand Total	Result	Indications
22 – 29	44 – 58	Low	Low scores indicate that you do not have much of a need for social approval from others.
30 – 36	59 – 73	Moderate	Moderate scores indicate that you have some need for social approval from others.
37 – 44	74 – 88	High	High scores indicate that you have a great need for social approval from others.

Social Situation Scale Descriptions

Teens scoring High on this scale tend to worry about meeting new people, feel embarrassed easily in social situations, try to avoid being in any social situations, and are self-conscious being in front of other people.

Social Perception Scale Descriptions

Teens scoring High on this scale tend to perceive how other people watch them and judge them. They worry about the opinions of others and are very worried about looking foolish to other people.

Social Situation and Social Perception Grand Total Descriptions

Teens scoring High on the Grand Total seek social approval from other people. When this happens they are self-conscious and feel worried in social situations. They perceive that others are watching and judging them, and are constantly concerned that they are making an unfavorable impression.

Social Approval

Events Where I Feel Anxious

Make a list of the social events in which you feel you might have intense anxiety or feel panicky. These events can be at home, school, workplace, or anywhere.

Answer the following questions to identify how much effort you are making to avoid social events that might cause you anxiety. USE NAME CODES.

Social Events I Avoid	Why I Avoid Them	What I Miss or Lose by Avoiding Them
Example: Parties.	I might act or say something in a way that people will judge me.	I miss being with my friends who do attend these parties.

Which events are the easiest to avoid? _____
_____
_____

When is it most difficult? Why? _____
_____
_____

People with Whom I Feel Anxious

Being around certain people can also cause anxiety. Make a list of the people in whose presence you begin to feel anxious, panicky, or worried. These people can be at home, in school, in the workplace, or anywhere.

Answer the following questions to identify how much effort you are making to avoid the people who make you anxious. USE NAME CODES.

People I Avoid	Why I Avoid Them	What I Miss or Lose by Avoiding This Person
Example: KLP	When he gets angry he often takes it out on me.	Opportunities for bonding and a better family life.

Which people are the easiest to avoid? Why? _____

_____

_____

Which are the most difficult? Why? _____

_____

_____

Social Approval

Situations Where I Feel Anxious

Make a list of the situations in which you have been very anxious, panicked, or worried. These situations can be at home, in school, at work, or anywhere.

Answer the following questions to identify how much effort you are exerting to avoid the situations that cause you to feel anxiety. USE NAME CODES.

People I Avoid	Why I Avoid Them	What I Miss by Avoiding This Situation
Example: Staying after school for the Chess Club.	I get picked on and bullied because there is a lack of teacher supervision.	I miss not having a chance to compete in tournaments with the club.

What can you do instead of avoiding the situation(s) above? (**Example:** *Speak in confidentiality with an authority at school about having more supervision at the Chess Club.*)

_____

_____

_____

_____

Ways I Avoid Social Situations

Many people will go to extreme lengths to avoid social situations.

Think about some of the things you do to avoid social situations and complete the table below. USE NAME CODES.

Ways I Avoid Social Situations	How I Do This	The Positive and/or Negative Results of Avoidance
Example: *I avoid bringing attention to myself.*	*At dances I sit in the corner and talk with a few close friends.*	*If I do this, I don't get anxious and people don't judge my dancing ability. But I get bored and would like to dance.*
Avoid bringing attention to myself.		
Remove myself from the situation.		
Use substances to be more social.		
Over-prepare and rehearse.		
Think about other things		
Focus on others, not myself.		
Other		

Which is your primary method of dealing with social situations? _____

_____

_____

What positive steps would you like to take to improve your social situations? _____

_____

_____

Social Situation Realities

People often over-exaggerate the negative impact of social situations in which they find themselves. It is important to carefully examine how you interact and perform in social situations

Think of a social situation in which you recently found yourself and then answer the questions. USE NAME CODES.

The Situation: _____
_____
_____

What was your concern about what might happen? _____
_____
_____
_____

Did it happen? _____
_____
_____
_____

If so, what was the worst thing about it? _____
_____
_____
_____

If not, what actually happened? _____
_____
_____
_____

Was your concern as valid as your thoughts? _____
_____
_____
_____

Need for Approval

People who experience a great deal of anxiety, especially in social situations, often feel a tremendous need for approval. In the spaces that follow, explore your need for approval from others. **Think about how you think, feel, and act when other people are present. USE NAME CODES.**

Why I Want Approval	Think	Feel	Act
Example: I want to be liked by everyone.	If I disagree with my friends they will not want to spend time with me.	I feel anxious - like I'm walking on eggshells all the time.	I do whatever my friends want to do.
I want to be liked by everyone.			
I seek positive feedback from others.			
I don't have the confidence I need.			
I believe that others are better than I am.			
I feel different from other people			
I depend on others for my self-worth.			
Other			
Other			

Why do you think you feel this way? Give an example. _____

_____

_____

Social Approval

Validation

Although everyone likes to be validated, it is helpful to let go of the notion of needing validation for who you are as a person or for your life choices. Now is the time to believe you are good enough without needing other people to validate this fact.

**For the following activity, complete each of the sentence starters below.
USE NAME CODES.**

The people I want to validate my choices, or who I am, are …

These people are important because …

The choices I have made because of the need for validation include …

I want _____ to say I'm okay because …

Upcoming choices I want to make because they are best for me include …

I will ensure that I am making decisions that are best for me by…

> *When we consistently suppress and distrust our intuitive knowingness, looking instead for authority, validation, and approval from others, we give our personal power away.*
> ~ **Shakti Gawain**

I'm Good Enough!

Teens who feel anxiety associated with looking good in the eyes of others often feel as if whatever they do is not enough. This belief is a negative, internal statement that you might be telling yourself often.

In the table that follows, identify those people whom you believe are constantly judging you negatively. This may be one person or several people, someone whose name you know or do not know - a teacher, a group, your family, etc. USE NAME CODES.

Ways I Think People Perceive Me	The Reality About Me	How I Can Think About This
Example: Some of my peers think I'm weird because I won't drink alcohol.	I really don't need alcohol to feel good!	I need to do what I need to do. I can explain it to my friends and let them think whatever.

What steps can you take to let go and accept that what you think about yourself is most important. ___

_____
_____
_____
_____

Social Approval

Rejection, Abandonment, and Disapproval

Many people who have problems with social anxiety have underlying fears of rejection, abandonment, and disapproval.

Identify three of your fears and answer the questions below to explore the levels of each of them. Place an X on the lines below of each of your fears. USE NAME CODES.

MY FEAR: _____

0 _____ **10**
(Not Very Fearful)   *(Very Fearful)*

How does this fear affect you in your daily life? _____

_____

_____

_____

MY FEAR: _____

0 _____ **10**
(Not Very Fearful)   *(Very Fearful)*

How does this fear affect you in your daily life? _____

_____

_____

_____

MY FEAR: _____

0 _____ **10**
(Not Very Fearful)   *(Very Fearful)*

How does this fear affect you in your daily life? _____

_____

_____

_____

Challenge Negative Thinking

People who suffer from social anxiety most often experience a wide variety of negative or possibly unrealistic thoughts that keep repeating in their heads.

Think about a social situation in which you find yourself experiencing intense anxiety.

Name that social situation: _____

_____

_____

Complete the table below.

Negative and/or Unrealistic Thoughts	Is This Thought Negative, Unrealistic, or Both?	Analyze and Challenge These Thoughts
Example: If I join the choir I won't know anyone there.	☒ Negative ☒ Unrealistic	I may not know anyone yet but it will be easy to make friends during rehearsal, car-pooling, etc.
	☐ Negative ☐ Unrealistic	
	☐ Negative ☐ Unrealistic	
	☐ Negative ☐ Unrealistic	
	☐ Negative ☐ Unrealistic	
	☐ Negative ☐ Unrealistic	
	☐ Negative ☐ Unrealistic	

Social Approval

Ways Thinking Can Be Debilitating

Often, people who have anxiety issues, may have thinking that is unhelpful and debilitating.

Respond to each of the four types of thinking and whether or not you tend to think like this at times. Then, describe times you have experienced these types of thoughts.

1. **Personalizing: Making the assumption that others are negatively focusing on you.**
   Example: Someone looks at you in a curious way and you assume it is negative.

   _____
   _____
   _____

2. **Catastrophizing: Blowing things way out of proportion.**
   Example: If someone notices that you are a bit anxious, it would be terrible.

   _____
   _____
   _____

3. **Predicting the Future: Assuming the worst.**
   Example: "Knowing" that when you will speak in class, you will be anxious and tremble.

   _____
   _____
   _____

4. **Mind-Reading: Assuming that you know exactly what other people are thinking.**
   Example: Because you know you tend to be anxious, they will view you as anxious.

   _____
   _____
   _____

What did you learn about yourself from the above types? What can you do about it?

_____
_____
_____

Positive Self-Talk Scripts

One aspect of people who need social approval is that they fear a negative thought in their head and then other negative thoughts build on the original one until the negative thoughts accumulate and the person shuts down.

For the following activity, identify which negative thought often begins your negative thinking in a social situation and then list other thoughts that follow:

> Original Thought:
>
> Other Thoughts That Follow:

Now list some positive thoughts that you could immediately use to counteract your negative thoughts from building.

> Original Thought:
>
> Other Thoughts That Follow:

Social Approval

Meet New People

People with social approval and social anxiety issues often have a difficult time making new friends and developing new relationships.

What are some ways you can get involved in activities to meet new friends in a safe way? USE NAME CODES.

Places to Meet New People	How I Can Accomplish This	Advantages
Example: In school.	Ask classmates to form a study group.	Make friends with people who have interests similar as mine.
School		
Clubs		
Organizations		
Volunteering		
Work		
Athletic Events		
Religious/Spiritual Activites		
Artistic Events		
Social Media		
Other		

Which options seems to be the best for you? Why? _____

_____

_____

Self-Appreciation

Many people seek approval from others because they do not appreciate themselves enough. You need to take time to appreciate yourself.

In the spaces that follow write words, doodle, or attach cutouts from magazines about some of the things you appreciate about yourself and how you show yourself this appreciation.

I appreciate my ...	I appreciate how I ...

I appreciate that I am ...	I show my appreciation for who I am by ...

Now share your work with others.

Social Approval

Accepting ME

A primary step to overcoming your need for social approval is to accept yourself for who you are and not try to be someone or something else.

In the spaces that follow, identify how you accept yourself for who you are.

Situations	Ways I Accept Myself	How I Am Able to Use This Aspect of Myself
Example: At School.	I am a great math tutor!	If others need help in math, I can help them with their homework, and perhaps they can help me with my literature assignments.
At School		
At Home		
In My Community		
In Social Situations		
Other		
Other		

MODULE IV

Perfectionism

Perfectionism is not the same thing as striving to be our best. Perfectionism is not about healthy achievement and growth; it's a shield.

~ Brene Brown

Name _____

Date _____

Module IV – Take-Away Skills

We have included skills for most of the handouts in each Module, *Conditions and Behavior* (1), *Frequency and Duration* (2), and/or *Accomplishment* (3) statements for each activity may be used in educational and/or treatment planning, and also used to measure progress toward goals. These Take-Away skills promote real life outcomes and behavioral changes. Feel free to add additional skills for each activity.

Examples

1. **Conditions and Behavior** – a skill or healthy habit to replace a previous less effective behavior/habit.
    - Now, I … *(less effective or undesired behavior)*
      when I … *(when do I do this?)*.
      Instead I will … *(more effective or desired new behavior)* in ___ out of ___ opportunities.
2. **Frequency and Duration** – a skill or healthy habit not necessarily tied to a condition or previous behavior.
    - I will *(describe the behavior)* _____ times per _____.
3. **Accomplishment** – an outcome that is a one-time accomplishment.
    - I will *(describe the accomplishment)* by _____ *(date)*.

Take-Away Skills Examples

Criticizing Myself..92
Conditions and Behavior
- Now, I … *beat myself up*
  when I … *don't get all A's in my classes.*
  Instead I will … *don't get all A's in my classes.*

Criticizing Others..93
Conditions and Behavior
- Now, I … *get mad at my sister*
  when … *she does not do chores the same way I do.*
  Instead I will … *thank her for doing her part, in 4 out of 4 opportunities.*

Handling Criticism from Others 94
Conditions and Behavior
- Now, I … *"check out"*
  when … *my teacher criticizes me.*
  Instead I will … *remind myself that he is here to help me and stay tuned in in 4 out of 4 opportunities.*

Perfectionistic Thinking 95
Conditions and Behavior
- Now, I … *fixate on what I "should" have done*
  when I … *do something I am not proud of.*
  Instead I will … *remind myself that everyone makes mistakes and move on in 4 out of 4 opportunities.*
- Now, I … *label myself as a failure*
  when I … *receive feedback from my teacher.*
  Instead I will … *accept the feedback as a learning tool, in 4 out of 4 opportunities.*

Perfectionism

Take-Away Skills Examples *(Continued)*

How I Feel When I Am Being a Perfectionist 96
Conditions and Behavior
- Now, I … *become crabby*
  when I … *am striving to be perfect.*
  Instead I will … *take three deep breaths to clear my head in 4 out of 4 opportunities.*

I Must Be Perfect 98
Conditions and Behavior
- Now, I … *don't turn in my work*
  when I … . *am worried that it is not good enough.*
  Instead I will … *accept that I did my best and turn it in, in 4 our of 4 opportunities.*

Perfectionistic Affirmations 99
Accomplishment
- I will … *make a collage honoring my positive qualities, by March 31st.*
Frequency and Duration
- I will … *tell myself a realistic affirmation 1 time every morning for 1 month.*

A Perfectionistic Contract 100
Accomplishment
- I will … *agree to do the best I can without needing to be perfect and sign the Perfectionistic Contract by the end of the month.*
Conditions and Behavior
- Now, I … *procrastinate*
- when I … *have to submit a paper.*
  Instead I will … *refer to my Perfectionistic Contract and turn it in in 4 out of 4 opportunities.*

Small Steps in Setting Realistic Goals 103
Frequency and Duration
- I will … *apply for one position each week for a month, as a means toward achieving my goal of getting a job.*

My Perfectionistic Moments 104
Conditions and Behavior
- Now, I … *do not turn in my papers on time*
  when I … *am afraid that they're not "A" worthy.*
  Instead I will … *begin sooner and turn them in on time in 4 out of 4 opportunities.*
- Now, I … *say "no" out of fear that I will not be "good" at it*
  when … *my friend asks me to go rock climbing.*
  Instead I will … *say "yes" and try it anyway, in 4 out of 4 opportunities.*
Frequency and Duration
- I will … *try one new sport one time every month for three months.*
- I will … *do one thing I have avoided doing because of my fear of being "bad" at it, one time a week for a month.*

The Positive Me 106
Frequency and Duration
- I will … *write down five things I am grateful for every day for a week.*
- I will … . *write two things I like about myself in a journal every day for a month.*

Perfectionism

Perfectionism Scale
Introduction and Directions

Perfectionism is a personality trait characterized by a person's striving for flawlessness and setting excessively high performance standards, accompanied by overly critical self-evaluations and concerns regarding others' evaluations.

Teens often perceive perfectionism as something positive and admirable. This is true to a certain point, but beyond that it can cause tremendous self-induced stress and anxiety. Perfectionism often creates an unhealthy need to set unrealistic standards, to work toward unachievable goals, to fear making mistakes, and to be critical of self and others.

This self-assessment contains 24 statements designed to help you explore if and how you tend to be perfectionistic. Read each item carefully and decide how much the statement describes you. In each of the choices listed, circle the number of your response.

In the following example, the circled number 2 indicates the statement is True for the person completing the scale.

	True	NOT True
1. I am extremely critical of myself	(2)	1

This is not a test and there are no right or wrong answers. Do not spend too much time thinking about your answers. Your initial response will be the most true for you. Be sure to respond to every statement.

(Turn to the next page and begin.)

Perfectionism Scale

	True	NOT True
1. I am extremely critical of myself	2	1
2. I hate myself if I don't get everything right	2	1
3. I take myself very seriously	2	1
4. I am very reliable	2	1
5. I don't like to be criticized	2	1
6. I have an "all-or-nothing" approach	2	1

Scale C = _____

	True	NOT True
7. I delay projects because I'm concerned I can't do a perfect job	2	1
8. I tend to let myself down no matter how well I do	2	1
9. I expect the same standards I have for myself from those around me	2	1
10. I feel that everything in my life must be perfect	2	1
11. I believe that if I do anything in an average way would be shameful	2	1
12. My worth is tied to my accomplishments	2	1

Scale S = _____

	True	NOT True
13. I avoid answering questions because I may say something stupid	2	1
14. I believe mistakes are personal flaws	2	1
15. I focus on my mistakes, not accomplishments	2	1
16. I only think about my failures when looking at the past	2	1
17. I have a fear of not doing everything in a perfect way	2	1
18. I don't accept when others make mistakes	2	1

Scale M = _____

	True	NOT True
19. I become very upset when I do not reach my goals	2	1
20. I set unrealistic goals for myself	2	1
21. I set unrealistic goals for others	2	1
22. I feel that anything less than meeting a goal perfectly is a total failure	2	1
23. I drive myself to reach higher standards	2	1
24. I want to be the best in every single thing I do	2	1

Scale G = _____

Go to the Scoring Directions

Perfectionism

Perfectionism Scale
Scoring Directions

Perfectionism creates a set of self-defeating thought patterns that push you to try to achieve unrealistically high goals.

The *Perfectionism Scale* is designed to help you figure out in which way you are perfectionistic and explore some ways you tend to create your own anxiety. On the scale, add the numbers that you circled in each section and write the scores on each of the TOTAL lines. You will receive a total in the range from 6 to 12. Then, transfer those numbers to the space below.

    C   Critical Total   = _____

    S   Standards Total   = _____

    M   Mistakes Total   = _____

    G   Goals Total   = _____

Profile Interpretation

Individual Total	Result	Indications
6 – 7	Low	If you scored in the LOW range, you do not show many perfectionistic traits.
8 – 10	Moderate	If you scored in the MODERATE range, you show some perfectionistic traits.
11 – 12	High	If you scored in the HIGH range, you show many perfectionistic traits.

Scale Descriptions

Critical – Teens scoring high on this scale are very critical about themselves and other people.

Standards – Teens scoring high on this scale set performance standards that are unrealistic and often unachievable.

Mistakes – Teens scoring high on this scale want to be flawless and never make a mistake.

Goals – Teens scoring high on this scale set unrealistic goals for themselves and for other people.

Criticizing Myself

Some people often set very high standards for themselves and then they are critical of themselves when they are unable to achieve their goals. They never feel as if they are good enough or doing enough.

Complete the table to explore when you tend to be self-critical and if you are too self-critical. In the third column, make an action plan to be less self-critical.
USE NAME CODES.

When do you tend to be critical of yourself?	Are you being too critical of yourself in this situation? Explain	What action plan can you have to be less critical of yourself?
Example: When I do not get an A in every one of my classes.	Maybe. I don't need all A's to get into the college I want to attend.	I have to remember that nobody is perfect!.

> *I'm always criticizing and only see the mistakes.*
> ~ David Chang

Does this quote apply to you? How? _____

_____

_____

To whom else in your life does this quote apply? Why? _____

_____

_____

Criticizing Others

At one time or another, all people find themselves in positions where they will be evaluating, and possibly criticizing, other people. Perfectionists tend to be very critical about others and are often harsh and judgmental in their criticisms.

Complete the table that follows to explore from whom you receive criticism, how you handle it, and how you could handle it better. USE NAME CODES.

With whom are you very critical?	Why are you critical of this person?	How can you perceive this person differently?
Example: My little sister.	I just want her to do well.	I can see that she's growing up and needs my support more than my criticism.

> *Every human being is entitled to courtesy and consideration. Constructive criticism is not only to be expected but sought.*
> ~ **Margaret Chase Smith**

What is constructive criticism? _____

_____

When you are critical, is it constructive? Explain. _____

_____

Pick an example of the last time you were critical of someone from your response above. Was that constructive criticism? Explain _____

_____

Managing Anxiety Workbook for Teens

Handling Criticism from Others

Constructive criticism can help a person to become more self-aware. It assists in identifying ways to improve one's performance. Many people who are perfectionistic view constructive criticism as unwelcome, react defensively, and then become even more self-critical.

Complete the table that follows to explore from whom you receive criticism, how you handle it, and how you could handle it better. USE NAME CODES.

From whom do you receive criticism?	How do you handle the criticism?	What are the ways you can handle the criticism better?
Example: My teacher.	I become angry and tune her out.	I need to accept that she knows what she is talking about and that she is trying to help me.

> *Criticism may not be agreeable, but it is necessary. It fulfils the same function as pain in the human body. It calls attention to an unhealthy state of things.*
>
> **~ Winston Churchill**

What are your thoughts about the above quotation? _____

_____

_____

Perfectionism

Perfectionistic Thinking

Perfectionistic thinking comes in many different forms. Some of the various forms are described below.

For each one, think about if and how you exhibit each type of thinking and provide examples from your daily life. Be honest with yourself! USE NAME CODES.

Should Statements *(Example: I should have done it better.)* _____

_____
_____
_____
_____
_____

Catastrophic Thinking *(Example: If I make a mistake, people will laugh at me and I will be humiliated.)* _____

_____
_____
_____
_____
_____

Over-Exaggerating *(Example: If I don't do this perfectly, my boss will fire me.)* _____

_____
_____
_____
_____
_____

All-or-Nothing Thinking *(Example: Everything I do must be absolutely perfect or it is no good.)* _____

_____
_____
_____
_____

> ***ASK YOURSELF: How is it possible to always do something perfectly when it's something new or unfamiliar, or when it involves uncertainty?***

How I Feel When I am Being a Perfectionist

People say they can recognize when they are being perfectionistic.
Through self-awareness, you can do the same.

Below, identify your negative feelings associated with your perfectionism.

How I Feel	How Will I Know	How I Can Reverse It
Example: Sad / Depressed.	I begin to feel tired and irritable.	I can look at the positive side and think about what I have to be grateful for.
Sad / Depressed		
Anxious		
Angry		
Frustrated		
Scared		
Other		

Which feeling do you experience most often when being perfectionistic?

People striving for excellence in a healthy way view mistakes as an opportunity to grow. They understand that they are part of the learning process and they accept them.

Consequences of perfectionism are that it inhibits one, keeps one from taking risks, reduces the ability to innovate and create, and stops playfulness and the desire to dream.

To which of the items in the above two paragraphs can you relate?

Perfectionism

Perfectionistic Thoughts

It is important to document the perfectionistic thoughts that pop into your head. Some of these might include such thoughts as *People will laugh at me*. Or *I'm a useless person if I don't reach my goals!*

In the thought bubbles, write some of your perfectionistic thoughts. USE NAME CODES.

What themes do you notice? _____

_____

_____

I Must Be Perfect

Many people feel that they must be perfect, or they will do everything in their power to try and be perfect. Think about the many ways in which you attempt to be perfect and how these ways limit you from what you want to achieve.

Think about the ways you attempt to be perfect. USE NAME CODES.

Ways I Seek Perfectionism	How I Try to Be Perfect	How These Ways Limit Me	How I Can Be Satisfied If I'm Not Perfect
Example: *Underachieving.*	*I don't try if I think I won't be perfect.*	*My grades will be affected.*	*It's easier and better to not try and fail than to try and work hard, and then fail.*
Underachieving			
Procrastination			
Being Too Cautious			
Checking for Mistakes			
Inability to take safe risks			
Worrying about small details			
Inability to try new things			

Perfectionism Affirmations

It can be helpful to create some realistic affirmations to remind you about perfectionism.

We've given you the first three. Create your own and/or brainstorm with others. Cut them out and put them on your refrigerator, tape them to your computer monitor, or stick them in your wallet, as reminders.

I don't have to be perfect!	I will do the best I can and hopefully finish on time!	The world has GREY Not just BLACK and WHITE

Managing Anxiety Workbook for Teens

A Perfectionistic Contract

By filling in the blanks on this contract, you will agree to live the rest of your life willing to do the best you can, and not always feeling the need to be perfect.

Complete the following contract and sign and date it. Keep it handy so that you can see it daily.

A Perfectionist Contract

I, _____, agree not to be perfectionist at home, with friends, or anywhere.
  NAME

I will try not to be perfectionistic by doing any of the following:

- I will not set standards that are too high. I will do this by:

  _____
  _____

- I will not be too critical of myself and others. I will do this by:

  _____
  _____

- I will not be angry or disappointed in myself when I make mistakes. I will do this by:

  _____
  _____

- I will not set goals that are too lofty to achieve. I will do this by:

  _____
  _____

_____ _____
NAME   **DATE**

Perfectionism

The Good and the Bad

People who exhibit perfectionistic tendencies have a difficult time realizing how these tendencies are harming them. They say things like *"I like to do things well"* and *"It makes me feel good."*

Below, based on your perfectionism, identify the ways it IS helpful to you, and the ways it IS NOT helpful to you.

My perfectionism is helpful to me …

My perfectionism is NOT helpful to me …

Which list is larger? Why? _____

_____

_____

Underlying Perfectionistic Reasons

Sometimes people who are perfectionistic have deep underlying reasons for thinking they must be perfect.

These questions will guide you through the process of uncovering these reasons. Think about why you are perfectionistic.

If I make a mistake, I think …

If I make a mistake, people will think …

If I don't reach very high standards, I will …

If I don't reach high standards, people will think …

If I don't reach my goals, I will …

If I don't reach my goals, people will think …

If I am criticized by others, I will …

- -

> *Striving for excellence motivates you; striving for perfection is demoralizing!*
> ~ **Harriet Braiker**

What are your thoughts about the above quotation?

Perfectionism

Small Steps in Setting Realistic Goals

If you are a perfectionist, you might set goals that are much too lofty for you or anyone to achieve. It is important that you take small steps in setting goals that are achievable, then set new goals. You will only get frustrated if you set unrealistic goals and are unable to achieve them. Breaking goals into small manageable steps helps.

In the steps that follow, set a long-term achievable goal and several short-term goals for one aspect of your life.

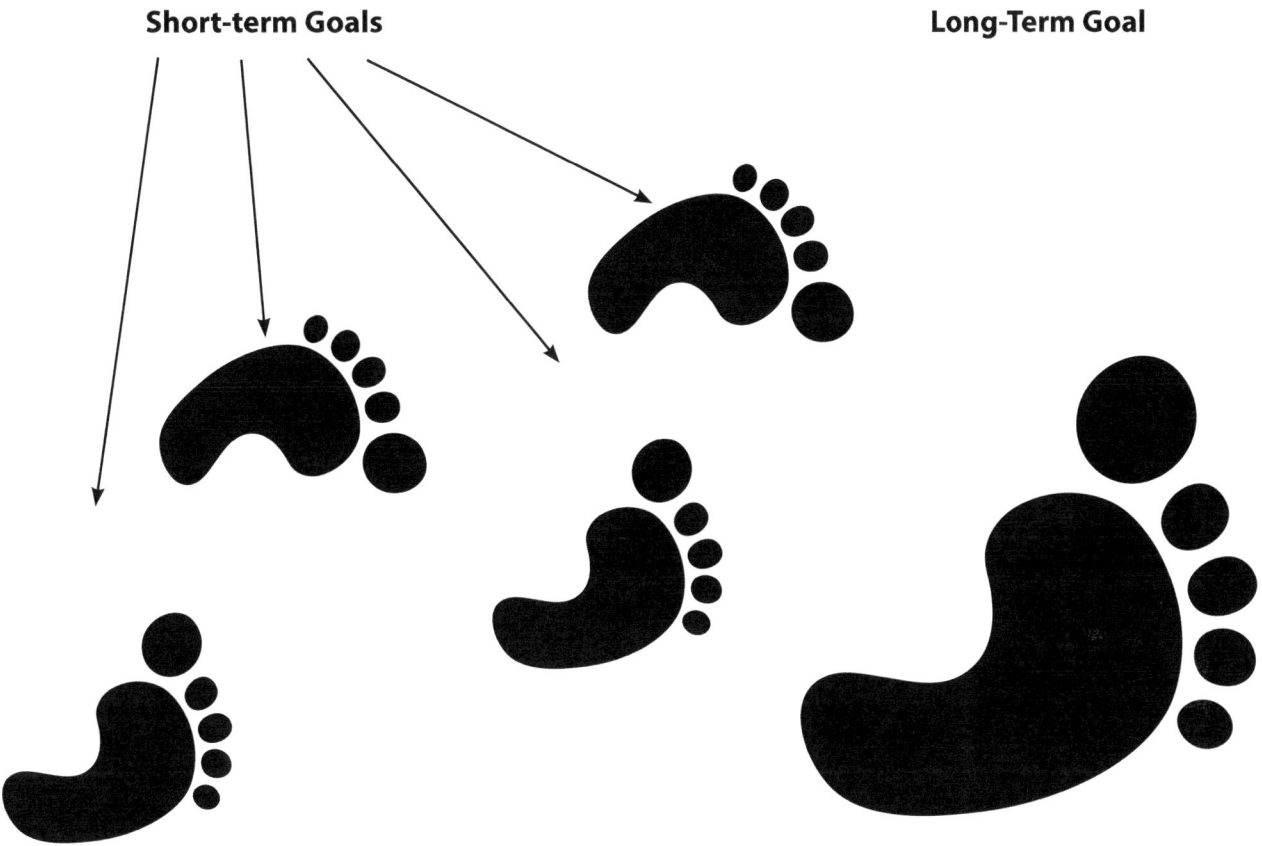

> *When it is obvious that the goals cannot be reached, don't adjust the goals, adjust the action steps.*
> ~ Confucius

How would the above quotation assist people who are perfectionists?

_____

_____

_____

My Perfectionistic Moments

It is important to understand the situations in which you tend to be perfectionistic and how this affects your daily functioning and relationships. **USE NAME CODES.**

What are some of the situations in which you feel like you are way too perfectionistic?

My Perfectionistic Moment Situation	Why I Feel or Act This Way	How It Affects Me & People Around Me	How I Could Be Less Perfectionistic
Example: I do not turn in group school projects until I check the details over again and again!	I worry that my work will have some mistakes and other people will blame me and think I'm worthless.	Others in the group get frustrated with me for taking so long to do my part.	After I check it over I could ask a group member I trust to double check my work.

Which situations are negatively affecting your life? _____

_____

_____

_____

Perfectionism

Respecting and Loving Myself

To overcome perfectionism, it is important to be aware of your love and respect for yourself.

In each of the blocks that follow, write words that describe your most positive qualities.
(Example: artistic, smart, compassionate, caring, good at soccer, etc.)

My People Skills

My Work / Volunteer Skills

My Personality Characteristics

My Special Gifts

The Positive Me

People who are perfectionistic thinkers tend to focus on their negative qualities and mistakes. However, they probably have many, many more positive qualities and successes than their negative qualities and failures.

Identify a negative quality, why you don't like it, and then list four positive qualities related to the negative one.

Settings	Things I Don't Like About Me Related to This Setting and Why	What I Do Like About Me Related to This Setting
My School Work	1.	1. 2. 3. 4.
My Home Life	1.	1. 2. 3. 4.
My Relationships	1.	1. 2. 3. 4.

Which aspects in the last column, do you like most about yourself and why? _____
_____
_____
_____

Save this page and post it somewhere in sight to remind yourself of your positive qualities.

MODULE V

Erasing the Stigma of Mental Health Issues

Stigma's power lies in silence. The silence that persists when discussion and action should be taking place …

~ **M. B. Dallocchio**

Name _____

Date _____

Erasing the Stigma of Mental Health Issues
Introduction

A stigma is extreme social disapproval of some type of personal characteristic or a belief that is not considered socially "acceptable." People who have a particular attribute considered unwanted by society are rejected or stigmatized as a result of the attribute. People who experience intense anxiety and panic attacks in the past are often judged unfairly to be "crazy," nervous, unrealistically worried, afraid around other people, phobic, and/or unstable. These judgments, or social stigmas, can cause people who experience these issues to feel devalued as human beings. They are often ostracized from activities, rejected in social situations, stereotyped, minimized in the workplace, and shunned by others. People experiencing the stigma of anxiety issues often feel extreme physical and psychological distress.

People who stigmatize and/or stereotype others bring about unfair treatment. This unfair treatment can be very obvious. For example, people make negative comments or laugh. On the other hand, this unfair treatment can be very subtle. For example, people assume that someone who experiences anxiety issues is fearful and nervous all the time, and they avoid or shun that person.

Stigmas affect a large percentage of people throughout the world. Some of the more common stigmas are associated with physical disabilities, mental health issues, age, body type, gender, sexual orientation, nationality, religion, family, ethnicity, race, religion, financial status, social subcultures, and conduct. Stigmas set people apart from society and produce feelings in them of shame and isolation. People who are stigmatized are often considered socially unacceptable and they suffer prejudice, rejection, avoidance, and discrimination.

WHAT CAN BE DONE?

Fear of judgment and ridicule about anxiety issues often compels individuals and their families to hide from society rather than face criticism, shunning, labeling, and stereotyping. Instead of seeking treatment, they struggle in silence. Let's discuss some ways you can combat the stereotypes and stigmas that are associated with these issues.

- You and your loved ones have choices. You can decide who is to know about your anxiety and what to tell them. You need not feel guilty, ashamed, or embarrassed.
- You are not alone. Remember that many other people are coping with a similar situation.
- Look into or start a support group to meet others who experience what you do.
- Seek help and remember that the activities in this workbook and treatment from medical professionals can help you to have a productive education and career, and to live a more satisfying life.
- Be proactive and surround yourself with supportive people – people you can trust. Social isolation is a negative side effect of the stigma linked to moodiness. Isolating yourself and discontinuing enjoyable activities will not help.

HOW CAN THIS SECTION HELP ME?

Managing Anxiety Workbook for Teens is designed to help you deal more effectively with your issues. This module is specifically designed to help you overcome the stigma attached to those issues. Complete the activities that follow to feel better about yourself, feel content, and become more resilient in the face of stress in your life.

Two Types of Mental Health Stigma

Mental health stigma can be divided into two types:

1. *Social stigma* is characterized by prejudicial attitudes and discriminating behavior directed towards individuals with mental health issues.

2. *Perceived stigma* is the internalizing by the people with mental health issues of their understanding of discrimination.

What do you think are the differences between these two types of stigmas?

_____
_____
_____
_____

Describe a time when you faced prejudice or discrimination because you experienced anxiety.

_____
_____
_____
_____

Describe a time when you felt like you were at a disadvantage because you experienced anxiety

_____
_____
_____
_____

Often one perceives others' stigmatizing, or exaggerates others' or their own reactions.

The Stigma of Intense Anxiety — THE PAST

People who experience anxiety in their lives are prone to recurring symptoms. When this happens, they can have a stigma placed on them by other people. Often the stigma attached to this issue stops one from moving forward - being unable to talk about it for fear of being judged or labeled. We can erase the stigma of any mental health issue by starting to discuss it with one person at a time and taking the time to explain the anxiety you lived through in the past.

Let's start with people with whom you have already shared your story.

With whom have you discussed your issues?	What did you say?	What was this person's reaction? What did the person say?	How did you feel?
Family			
Friends			
Acquaintances			
Teachers, Coaches and/or Other School Administrators			
School Counselor and/or Mental Health Professional			
Other			

If any one of the above reacted in a negative way, to what do you attribute that reaction?

_____

_____

_____

Erasing the Stigma of Mental Health Issues

The Stigma of Intense Anxiety — THE PRESENT

If you are yet to tell your story to people, now may be the time. This workbook has helped you to organize your thoughts and feelings about your anxiety. One of the ways to erase this stigma is to talk about it and let others know that people who are very anxious are just like anyone else who have some type of an issue.

Perhaps it is time to talk with other people whom you trust and/or feel safe.

Person with whom you might discuss your issue?	What would you say to this person?	What do you think this person's reaction might be?	What could you gain or lose by discussing it with this person?
Family			
Friends			
Acquaintances			
Teachers, Coaches and/or Other School Administrators			
School Counselor and/or Mental Health Professional			
Other			

Brainstorm this with the group:
    At what point, in a serious relationship, is it time to discuss your issues?

Speak Your Mind

> *Follow the path of the unsafe, independent thinker. Expose your ideas to the danger of controversy. Speak your mind and fear less the label of 'crackpot' than the stigma of conformity.*
>
> ~ **Thomas J. Watson**

What does the above quotation mean to you? _____

_____

_____

_____

_____

Do you ever speak your mind? Why or Why Not? _____

_____

_____

_____

_____

Are you worried about being labeled? Explain. _____

_____

_____

_____

_____

How can you expose your ideas to others? _____

_____

_____

_____

_____

What is keeping you from telling your story? _____

_____

_____

_____

_____

If We Stamp Out the Stigma …

If we stamp out the stigma attached to mental health issues, shed the shame and eliminate the fear, then we open the door for people to speak freely about what they are feeling and thinking.

~ **Jaletta Albright Desmond**

**Journal your thoughts about the quotation above,
and how you can do your part to erase the stigma of anxiety issues.**

_____
_____
_____
_____
_____
_____
_____
_____
_____
_____
_____
_____
_____
_____
_____
_____
_____
_____
_____
_____
_____

Glenn Close said …

The most powerful way to change someone's view is to meet them … People who do come out and talk about mental illness, that's when healing can really begin. You can lead a productive life.

Name a time when you have changed someone else's view – about anything. _____
_____
_____

How did that feel to you? _____
_____
_____

Name a time you were tempted to talk about your anxiety issues, but didn't? Why not? _____
_____
_____

Write about a situation in which you talked about your anxiety issues? _____
_____
_____
_____
_____

How did that feel?_____
How did it work out? _____
_____

Who is a trusted person you can talk with and begin to heal? _____
Anyone else?_____
Who is a trusted person you can ask for a referral of someone to talk with in order to begin to heal?_____
_____
Anyone else?_____
In an ideal world, how can you lead a more stable life?_____
_____
_____

How can you contribute to changing stigma?_____
_____
_____

Erasing the Stigma of Mental Health Issues

Effects of Anxiety Issues

Check out these harmful effects of the stigma of anxiety. USE NAME CODES. Write on the lines next to each item if it has affected you in some way and how.

1. Lack of understanding by family _____

2. Lack of understanding by friends _____

3. Lack of understanding by teachers and school personnel_____

4. Discrimination at school _____

5. Inability to join clubs and organizations_____

6. Inability to manage the anxiety_____

7. Pressure from friends _____

8. The belief that you will never be able to succeed or that you can't improve your situation.
_____

On the line of the corresponding number, write the name of a person you can speak to, a person who might help to support you as you face each of the situations you noted above. Add a reason you've chosen that person.

1. _____
2. _____
3. _____
4. _____
5. _____
6. _____
7. _____
8. _____

Managing Anxiety Workbook for Teens

The Stigma of Going to a Mental Health Therapist

Many people have pre-conceived ideas about anyone seeking therapy. USE NAME CODES.

Do you know of anyone who has gone to a mental health therapist? Write what you know about the experience. _____
_____
_____

Here are some facts about mental health and mental health therapy.

- Mental health includes how you act, feel, and think in different situations.
- Mental health problems can be caused by many different things including medical health issues, abuse (emotional, physical, verbal, sexual), stress, worry, loss of a relationship, food issues, ADHD, STDs, family changes, addictions, traumatic event, problems, wanting to build up self-confidence, etc.
- If someone goes to a mental health therapist, this does NOT mean the person is crazy. Mental health therapists treat people the same as any other medical doctor treats problems.
- There needs to be a good connection between you and the therapist. Your therapist should be someone you feel you can trust.
- This might take a few meetings and/or a few therapists, to find the right one for you.
- Non-judgmental people who truly care about you will not judge you in a negative way. They will be proud of you for seeking help.
- The therapist does not assume that you have a mental illness. The therapist assumes something is troubling you, knows that no one leads a perfect life, and admires you for trying to make changes in your life.
- The therapist's job is to help you understand what's going on.
- The therapist will not tell you how to live your life, or how to think, act, or believe.
- The therapist is not an advice-giver, but will help you think about how to increase your quality of life.
- The therapist may have some thoughts, and with you, will help you make changes.
- The therapist can help you to increase your life management skills.
- The therapist will help you recognize and express your feelings in a healthy way.
- The only person who can "fix" your problems is you, but a therapist will help you with an action plan.
- The mental health therapist may suggest that you see a medical doctor for medication.
- Therapy can be a slow or long process. Being open and honest, and wanting to feel better, will make the difference.

Place an X by the facts that you were not aware of.

What are your concerns about talking with a mental health therapist? _____
_____
_____

After learning about these facts, can you make a commitment to speak with a counselor or therapist?

*signature*_____

Will You Speak Out?

> *Ten people who speak make more noise than ten thousand who are silent.*
> ~ Napoleon Bonaparte

How can YOU speak out to erase the stigma about people who have a high level of anxiety?

_____
_____
_____
_____
_____
_____
_____
_____
_____
_____

Brainstorm with a few other people about how you can speak out to erase the stigma of a high level of anxiety?

_____
_____
_____
_____
_____
_____
_____
_____
_____
_____

My Negative Thoughts

You can begin to overcome the stigma related to anxiety issues by refusing to worry about what others think. When you are worried about what others say about you, or might say about you, you will have a difficult time enjoying life.

Explore and write about the negative thoughts that go through your head about others and what they think of you?

Others think I am …

Others don't think I can …

Others possibly find me …

I think others might be afraid or wary of me because …

Others label me as …

This makes me feel …

Now that you have written these thoughts, take a big heavy black marker and put a big **X** through all of the thoughts above. When these negative thoughts come into your head, picture that big X, reminding you not to worry about what others think.

Erasing the Stigma of Mental Health Issues

Focus on Your Strengths

You can do many things to help fight the stigma associated with your anxiety issues. You can focus on your strengths rather than your limitations. Demonstrate to others, and yourself, that you have a great deal to offer.

In the spaces that follow, identify some of your strengths. You have much to share, so take a few minutes to think about and write about some of your greatest strengths.

My strengths related to school:

_____

_____

My strengths related to relationships with family and friends:

_____

_____

My strengths related to my work or volunteer job:

_____

_____

My strengths related to creativity:

_____

_____

My strengths related to special skills I possess:

_____

_____

How can you share these strengths to show others that even though you may have anxiety issues, you are a capable, talented human being?

_____

_____

Ways I Try to Minimize My Anxiety Issues

Many people dealing with the stress that occurs from intense anxiety will try a variety of ways to minimize its stigma.

Complete the following table to explore the various ways in which you minimize your issues and how this makes you feel. Describe some better ways to cope.

Ways I Minimize the Stigma of Anxiety	The Effect This Has on Others and Myself	A Better Way to Cope
Example: *I pretend that nothing is wrong with me.*	*Others think I should just 'get over' my anxiety and move on. It's not that easy and it upsets me when they say that.*	*Explain that I've been having some anxiety issues and I'm working on learning how to manage them.*
I pretend that nothing is wrong with me.		
I don't ask for help.		
I say things like "Nothing can ever help me."		
I do not talk about my anxiety issues.		
I laugh and make jokes about my anxiety.		
I often avoid people.		
Other		
Other		

Erasing the Stigma of Mental Health Issues

Ways I Am Treated

Think about some of the ways that people treat you because of the symptoms you show due to your anxieties. In the spaces below, explore the various ways people treat you.

Write about those who treat you unfairly and why.

I am criticized by my family and/or friends …

I am ignored by my family and/or friends …

I encounter problems at work …

I encounter problems at home …

I am subjected to teasing or harassment …

I am laughed at …

I treat myself unfairly by …

I treat myself fairly by …

Self-Doubt

Don't let stigma of anxiety issues create self-doubt and shame. One of the most important ways to minimize this stigma is to explore how you doubt yourself. Self-doubt almost always stems from a lack of understanding or from past experiences, rather than information based on the facts. Feeling ashamed, embarrassed, or guilty because of what you experienced can be self-defeating.

How does the stress associated with living with anxiety issues cause you to doubt yourself? How can you control your self-doubt in a positive and strong way?

Ways I Doubt Myself	How This Negatively Affects Me	What I Can Do About it
Example: I am very anxious when I need to speak up in public.	I avoid it, and this is holding me back from participating in class.	I can practice with small groups until I build my confidence.

> *However you arrive at the ability to ignore self-doubt - if you can acquire it or possess it or find it or discover it – move beyond self-doubt.*
> ~ **Dwight Yoakum**

How do you relate to this quotation? _____

_____

Erasing the Stigma of Mental Health Issues

A Poster about the STIGMA of People Who Experience Anxiety

In the space that follows, draw a collage of pictures, symbols, and/or words, of how you believe you are being stigmatized by others.

A Poster about ACCEPTANCE of People who Experience Anxiety

In the space that follows, draw a collage of pictures, symbols, and/or words, of what you believe that the stress related to anxiety looks like when you are accepted.

DE-STIGMA-TIZE with the Facts about Mental Health Issues

Myth: Mental health issues are rare.
   Fact: Mental health issues are not rare and affect nearly everyone either directly or indirectly.

Myth: People with mental health issues are unable to lead successful, productive lives.
   Fact: Most people with a mental health issues respond to treatment, learn to cope with and manage their problems, and go on to lead productive and fulfilling lives.

Myth: People who have mental health issues will not get better.
   Fact: Once diagnosed, mental health issues are treatable. While they are not always cured, they can be managed effectively. Most people with mental health issues live productive and positive lives. Many receive therapy and medications. Individuals with severe or persistent mental health issues who do not respond well to therapy or meds may require more support, or different therapists or meds, and they do well; and some may not function as highly as others.

Myth: People with mental health problems are violent and unpredictable.
   Fact: While some people who suffer from mental health issues do commit antisocial acts, a mental health issue does not equal criminality or violence - despite the media's tendency to emphasize a suspected link. People with mental illness are no more likely to commit violence than anyone in the general public, but they are more likely to be victimized and are more likely to inflict violent actions on themselves.

Myth: Mental health issues happen because of bad parenting or personal weakness.
   Fact: The main risk factors for mental health issues are not bad parenting or personal weakness but rather genetics, severe and prolonged stress (such as physical or sexual abuse), or other environmental influences (such as birth trauma or head injury).

Myth: Treatments for mental health issues is not usually effective.
   Fact: The effectiveness of any treatment depends on a number of factors including the type of mental issue and the particular needs of the individual. A combination of psychiatric medication and psychotherapy, or social interventions are the most effective way to treat mental health issues.

Myth: Mental health issues are caused by everyday stressors.
   Fact: It may seem that stress is responsible for mental health issues; however, there is no one clear cause of mental health issues. Rather, it is a result of complex interactions between psychological, biological, genetic and social factors. Stress, stigma, and lack of support can make it worse for the individual.

Myth: Mental health issues are always hereditary.
   Fact: Some mental health issues include a genetic component, which results in a predisposition or vulnerability toward the illness among children and siblings, but environment also plays a key role in the development of certain mental health issues. If someone in one's family has mental health issues, that person will be at higher risk.

If you start to experience the symptoms of a mental health issue, it is important for you to see a medical professional to determine if you have a problem that will require treatment. If you know of anyone who seems to have symptoms of a mental health issue, urge that person to do the same.

Coping with the Stigma of an Anxiety Issue

Get treatment. Don't let the fear of being *labeled* with an anxiety issue prevent you from seeking help. Treatment can provide relief by identifying and reducing symptoms that interfere with your work and personal life. How can you get treatment? _____
_____
_____
_____

Don't let stigma create self-doubt and shame. If you are buying into the stigma, you will have the mistaken belief that your issue is a sign of personal weakness, or that *you should* be able to control it better. How can you have less self-doubt? _____
_____
_____
_____

How can you have less shame? _____
_____
_____
_____

Don't isolate yourself. Have the courage to confide in your family members, friends, school personnel, and respected members of your community. Whom can you reach out to and whom can you trust for the compassion, support, and understanding you need? _____
_____
_____
_____

Get help at work. If you are having a high level of anxiety and it is affecting your school work, talk confidentially with your counselor to find available plans and programs which might help. _____
_____
_____
_____

If you and others are willing, share responses.

A Letter to the Editor

Your openness can help instill courage in others who are facing anxiety issues, and it will help to educate the public about the effect that these issues have on you personally. Write a letter to the editor of your school or local newspaper about stigma. You will be speaking out for yourself and advocate for others who might have these issues.

TO: _____

_____

_____

_____

_____

_____

_____

_____

_____

_____

_____

_____

_____

_____

_____

_____

_____

_____

_____

_____

_____

_____

Signed _____

Whole Person Associates is the leading publisher of training resources for professionals who empower people to create and maintain healthy lifestyles. Our creative resources will help you work effectively with your clients in the areas of stress management, wellness promotion, mental health, and life skills.

Please visit us at our web site: **WholePerson.com**. You can check out our entire line of products, place an order, request our print catalog, and sign up for our monthly special notifications.

Whole Person Associates
800-247-6789
Books@WholePerson.com